BISON BOOKS

USES OF PLANTS BY THE INDIANS OF THE MISSOURI RIVER REGION

Melvin R. Gilmore

Foreword by Hugh Cutler

Illustrations by Bellamy Parks Jansen

ENLARGED EDITION

University of Nebraska Press
Lincoln and London

Foreword copyright © 1977 by the University of Nebraska Press
Drawings by Bellamy Parks Jansen © 1991 by Bellamy Parks Jansen

First Enlarged Edition paperback printing: 1991
Most recent printing indicated by the last digit below:
10   9   8   7   6   5   4

Library of Congress Cataloging-in-Publication Data
Gilmore, Melvin R. (Melvin Randolph), 1868–1940.
Uses of Plants by the Indians of the Missouri River region / Melvin R.
Gilmore; foreword by Hugh Cutler; Illustrations by Bellamy Parks Jansen.—
Enl. ed.
p.   cm.
Revision of the author's thesis, University of Nebraska, 1914.
Includes bibliographical references and index.
ISBN 0-8032-7034-8 (pbk.)
1. Indians of North America—Missouri River Valley—Ethnobotany.
2. Ethnobotany—Missouri River Valley.   3. Botany—Missouri River Val-
ley.   I. Title.
E99.M82G55   1991   90-25514
978'.00497—dc20   CIP

Reproduced from the Thirty-third Annual Report of the Bureau of American
Ethnology (Washington, D.C.: Government Printing Office, 1919). Thirty-
one drawings have been added to this Expanded Edition and some details
have been updated.

CONTENTS

ILLUSTRATIONS

vii

Drawings begin on p. 87

FOREWORD

Hugh Cutler
Missouri Botanical Garden

In this book, one of the classics in ethnobotany, Melvin R. Gilmore presents the Indians of the Northern Great Plains, their culture, and their environment as one active pattern—as elements of an evolutionary sequence. Gilmore wanted to show that primitive man and his culture were tied intricately with plants and the environment, an idea that is held by many anthropologists, archaeologists, and biologists today. He wanted also to demonstrate that many plants used by American Indians might fruitfully be cultivated by others. This, too, is an idea that has come into its own.

Gilmore was predisposed by his background and training to favor the evolutionary view and the ecological method: to study the way things change with time and the interrelatedness of things. Gilmore was born on March 11, 1868, in the small town of Valley, Nebraska; after completing the course of Fremont Normal School, he taught in Elk City and farmed with his father.[1] In 1903, preparing to become a missionary to Japan, he entered a school affiliated with the Christian Church, Cotner College, in Bethany, Nebraska, near Lincoln. There he taught ancient languages while finishing his A.B. After graduating in 1904 he stayed on at Cotner, teaching a range of biology courses, and began advanced study in botany and geography at the University of Nebraska. At the time, Dean Charles E. Bessey (1845–1915) had made the University an important center of botanical research. Bessey was an international authority on the phylogeny of flowering plants, and his graduate seminars produced some of the nation's leading botanists. A scholar of world-wide influence, he was botany editor of the journal *Science* for eighteen years and, in 1910–11, was president of the American Association for the Advancement of Science. He was among the first Americans to

---

[1] Biographical information about Gilmore is drawn from David Erickson, "Melvin Randolph Gilmore, Incipient Cultural Ecologist: A Biographic Analysis" (M.A. thesis, University of Nebraska–Lincoln, 1971) and from Volney H. Jones, obituary of Melvin R. Gilmore, *Chronica Botanica* 6 (1941): 219–21.

import from Europe the ecological approach to botany—the view
that plants should be studied in their relationships with other
living things as a community—and he stimulated renewed research on the vital subject of the classification of plants as it
relates to their evolution. Bessey also devoted himself to acquir-
ing a knowledge of the botany of Nebraska and to assisting the
farmers of the state with what he knew. Like Bessey, Gilmore
accepted an evolutionary view, used an ecological approach, and
wanted his research to have some practical use for the people of
Nebraska. Gilmore also studied with one of Bessey's best stu-
dents, the ecologist Frederic E. Clements (1874–1945), and he
learned the methods of anthropology from Addison E. Sheldon,
the first ethnographic fieldworker for the Nebraska State Historical Society. At a distance Gilmore became a protegé of James
Mooney of the Bureau of American Ethnology, upon whose advice,
in 1911, he was appointed curator of the State Historical Society
Museum.

By 1914 when Gilmore, at the age of forty-six, presented this
report as his thesis for the Ph.D. degree in botany at the University of Nebraska, he had seen many changes in life on the Plains.[2]
While he was a boy, the great buffalo herds were finished off, the
last Indian wars were fought, and the Indians confined to reservations—ranchers and cattle and farmers and grain fields spread
onto lands the Indians had once used. The Indians and their uses
of plants had changed as time passed, and plants and people
changed as they moved from one region to another. Indians who
had lived in eastern forests modified their ways of obtaining food,
shelter, clothing, and medicine when they moved west to open
prairies and plains, yet vestiges of their old habits persisted in
names, food preferences, and customs.

In 1914 very few of the Indians still lived on their old lands,
and the plants they had once gathered were far away or scarce
because cattle and farms had destroyed them. But many of the old
Indians Gilmore interviewed had lived with the plants and
gathered them in the days before food was distributed by Indian
agents on the reservations, and they still knew the old names,
uses, and symbolism. The few introduced species mentioned by
Gilmore exemplify how the culture of the Indians was adapted to
new elements in their environment. The watermelon, for example,
had been introduced from Europe so soon after the Spanish and

[2] It was published in the Thirty-third Annual Report of the Bureau of American
Ethnology in 1919, but some copies carry in addition a printed thesis title page
dated 1914.

French reached the Americas that its origins were forgotten. The South American and Mexican squashes (*Cucurbita maxima* and *C. moschata*), which reached the Missouri River region in the 1880s, were grown and used in the same ways as native squashes and pumpkins, and were soon simply grouped with ancient foods.

Gilmore left the Nebraska State Historical Society in 1916 to become curator of the museum of the State Historical Society of North Dakota; from there, in 1923, he moved to the Museum of the American Indian, Heye Foundation; and in 1929 he became curator of ethnology at the Museum of Anthropology of the University of Michigan, where he remained until his death in 1940. At Michigan, Gilmore extended his studies to encompass plant material sent to him from many archaeological sites, most of them in the United States, always with the intention of defining relationships between nature and culture. His work was carried on by his principal student and associate, Volney H. Jones, who succeeded him in his post at Michigan.

Uses of Plants by the Indians of the Missouri River Region is essential to an understanding of how the Plains Indians lived on the land. Since 1914, other scholars have published works that add to what Gilmore had discovered. George F. Will and George R. Hyde, in their *Corn Among the Indians of the Upper Missouri* (1917; rptd. Lincoln: University of Nebraska Press, 1964), thank Gilmore for seed and information and give an excellent comparative account of the Indians' use of corn. They also draw upon the work of Gilbert L. Wilson, especially his *Agriculture of the Hidatsa Indians: An Indian Interpretation* (University of Minnesota Studies in the Social Sciences, no. 9 [Minneapolis, 1917]).

Many of the plants of the Missouri River region are included in Paul A. Vestal and Richard E. Schultes, *The Economic Botany of the Kiowa Indians As It Relates to the History of the Tribe* (Cambridge: Botanical Museum of Harvard University, 1939). An important series on the ethnobotany of Indians in Wisconsin was written by Huron H. Smith and published by the Public Museum of the City of Milwaukee. Smith's *Ethobotany of the Menomini Indians* (1923; rptd. Westport, Conn.: Greenwood Press, 1970) is useful for comparisons with the Winnebago Indian data which Gilmore published. Richard A. Yarnell, a student of Volney Jones's and thus an offshoot of Gilmore's teaching, has published a survey, *Aboriginal Relationships Between Culture and Plant Life in the Upper Great Lakes Region* (Anthropological Papers, Museum of Anthropology, University of Michigan [Ann Arbor, 1964]).

Many of the scientific names for plants which Gilmore used cannot be found in recent floras, such as Theodore Van Bruggen, *The Vascular Plants of South Dakota* (Ames: Iowa State University Press, 1976), or Julian A. Steyermark, *Flora of Missouri* (Ames: Iowa State University Press, 1963), although many of them can be identified by their common names. Gilmore used the publications of P. Axel Rydberg, an alumnus of the University of Nebraska who taught at Luther College in Wahoo, Nebraska. Most of Gilmore's plants can be found in Rydberg's *Flora of the Prairies and Plains of Central North America,* revised edition (New York: New York Botanical Garden, 1932). For the convenience of the reader, I have appended a list of those scientific names used by Gilmore that have changed since his day, showing their recent equivalents; and I have added an index to scientific and common names used in the book. The most recent authority for the flora in the plains region is T. M. Barkley et al., eds., *Flora of the Great Plains* (Lawrence: University Press of Kansas, 1986).

Scientific Names Used by Gilmore and Recent Equivalents

xviii	Apios tuberosa	Indian Potato
	= *Apios americana* Medic.	
7	*Salsola pestifer*	Russian Thistle
	= *S. iberica* Senn. & Pau.	
7	*Leontodon taraxacum*	Dandelion
	= *Taraxacum officinale* Weber	
7	*Roripa armoracia*	Horseradish
	= *Armoracia rusticana* (Lam.) Gaertner	
10	*Polystictus versicolor* (L.) Fr.	Bracket Fungus
	= *Coriolus versicolor* (L. ex Fr.) Quél.	
10	*Lycoperdon gemmatum* Batsch.	Puffball
	= *L. perlatum* Pers.	
11	*Parmelia borreri* Turn.	Lichen
	= *P. subrudecta* Nyl.	
11	*Usnea barbata* Hoffm.	Lichen
	= *U. hirta* (L.) Wigg.	
11	*Pinus murrayana* Oreg. Com.	Lodgepole Pine
	= *P. contorta* Dougl. var. *latifolia* Engelm. ex Wats.	
14	*Spartina michauxiana* Hitchc.	Slough Grass
	= *S. pectinata* Link.	
14	*Savastanta odorata* (L.) Scribn.	Sweet Grass
	= *Hierochloë odorata* (L.) Beauv.	
16	*Andropogon furcatus* Muhl.	Big Bluestem
	= *A. gerardii* Vitman	
18	*Tradescantia virginica* L.	Spiderwort, Spider Lily
	= *T. occidentalis* (Britt.) Smyth	

19	*Allium mutabile* Michx.	Wild Onion
	= *A. canadense* L.	
19	*Lilium umbellatum* Pursh	Lily
	= *L. philadelphicum* L.	
20	*Iris versicolor* L.	Blue Flag
	= *I. virginica* L.	
20	*Populus sargentii* Dode.	Cottonwood
	= *P. deltoides* Marsh. subsp. *monilifera* (Ait.) Eckenw.	
21	*Salix interior* Rowlee	Sandbar Willow
	= *Salix exigua* Nutt. subsp. *interior* (Rowlee) Cronq.	
22	*Hicoria ovata* (Mill.) Britton	Hickory Nut
	= *Carya ovata* (Mill.) K. Koch	
23	*Quercus rubra* L.	Red Oak
	= *Q. borealis* Michx. f.	
24	*Ulmus fulva* Michx.	Slippery Elm, Red Elm
	– *U. rubra* Muhl	
24	*Toxylon pomiferum* Raf.	Osage Orange, Bois d'Arc
	= *Maclura pomifera* (Raf.) Schneid.	
25	*Humulus americana* Nutt.	Hops
	= *H. lupulus* L.	
25	*Urtica gracilis* Ait.	Nettle
	= *U. dioica* L.	
26	*Allionia nyctaginea* Michx.	Wild Four-O'Clock
	= *Mirabilis nyctaginea* (Michx.) MacMill.	
27	*Nymphaea advena* Soland.	Large Yellow Pond Lily
	= *Nuphar luteum* (L.) Sibth. & Sm.	
28	*Pulsatilla patens* (L.) Mill.	Pasque Flower, Twin-flower
	= *Anemone patens* L.	
32	*Grossularia missouriensis* (Nutt.) Cov. & Britt.	Wild Gooseberry
	= *Ribes missouriense* Nutt.	
32	*Fragaria americana* (Porter) Britton	Wild Strawberry
	= *F. vesca* L. var. *americana* Porter	
32	*Rubus strigosus* Michx.	Wild Raspberry
	= *R. idaeus* L. subsp. *sachalinensis* (Levl.) Focke var. sachalinensis	
33	*Rosa pratincola* Greene	Wild Rose
	= *R. arkansana* Porter	
34	*Malus ioensis* (Wood) Britton	Crab Apple
	= *Pyrus ioensis* (Wood) Carruth	
35	*Crataegus chrysocarpa* Ashe	Red Haw
	= *C. rotundifolia* Moench	
36	*Prunus besseyi*	Sand Cherry
	= *P. pumila* L. var. *besseyi* (Bailey) Gl.	
36,37	*Padus nana* (DuRoi) Roemer	Chokecherry
	and *Padus melanocarpa* (A. Nelson) Shafer	Western Chokecherry
	= *Prunus virginiana* L.	
37	*Acuan illinoensis* (Michx.) Kuntze	Spider-bean
	= *Desmanthus illinoensis* (Michx.) MacMill.	
38	*Baptisia bracteata* Ell.	Black Rattle-pod
	= *B. bracteata* Muhl. ex Ell. var. *glabrescens* (Larisey) Isely	

39   *Astragalus caroliniana* L.   Little Rattle-pod
       = *A. canadensis* L.
39   *Geoprumnon crassicarpum* (Nutt.) Rydb.   Buffalo Pea,
                                                                  Ground Plum

       = *Astragalus crassicarpus* Nutt.
42   *Parosela enneandra* (Nutt.) Britton   Prairie Clover
       = *Dalea enneandra* Nutt.
42   *Parosela aurea* (Nutt.) Britton   Prairie Clover
       = *Dalea aurea* Nutt. ex Pursh
42   *Petalostemon purpureum* (Vent.) Rydb.   Purple Prairie Clover
       = *Dalea purpurea* Vent.
42   *Petalostemon candidum* (Willd.) Michx.   White Prairie Clover
       = *Dalea candida* Michx. ex Willd.
42   *Glycine apios* L.   Indian Potato
       = *Apios americana* Medic.
43   *Falcata comosa* (L.) Kuntze   Ground Bean
       = *Amphicarpaea bracteata* (L.) Fern.
46   *Lathyrus ornatus* Nutt.   Wild Sweet Pea
       = *L. polymorphus* Nutt.
46   *Ionoxalis violacea* (L.) Small   Sheep Sorrel, Violet Wood Sorrel
       = *Oxalis violacea* L.
46   *Xanthoxalis stricta* (L.) Small   Yellow Wood Sorrel
       = *Oxalis stricta* L.
46   *Linum lewisii* Pursh   Wild Flax
       = *L. perenne* L. var. *lewisii* (Pursh) Eat. & Wright
47   *Chamaesyce serpyllifolia* (Pers.) Small   Spurge
       = *Euphorbia serpyllifolia* Pers.
47   *Dichrophyllum marginatum* (Pursh) Kl. & Garcke   Snow-on-the-
                                                                     mountain
       = *Euphorbia marginata* Pursh
48   *Toxicodendron toxicodendron* (L.) Britton Poison Oak, Poison Ivy
       = *T. rydbergii* (Small) Greene
       (= *Rhus radicans* L.)
49   *Impatiens biflora* Walt.   Wild Touch-me-not
       = *I. capensis* Meerb.
51   *Malvastrum coccineum* (Pursh) A. Gray   Red False Mallow
       = *Sphaeralcea coccinea* (Pursh) Rydb.
51   *Nuttallia nuda* (Pursh) Greene   Blazing Star
       = *Mentzelia nuda* (Pursh) T. & G.
52   *Opuntia humifusa* Raf.   Prickly Pear
       = *O. polyacantha* Haw.
54   *Lepargyrea argentea* (Nutt.) Greene   Buffalo-berry
       = *Shepherdia argentea* Nutt.
55   *Washingtonia longistylis* (Torr.) Britton   Sweet Cicely
       = *Osmorhiza longistylis* (Torr.) DC.
55   *Heracleum lanatum* Michx.   Cow-Parsnip, Beaver Root
       = *H. sphondylium* L. subsp. *montanum* (Schleich.) Briq.
55   *Cogswellia daucifolia* (Nutt.) M.E. Jones   Love Seed
       = *Lomatium foeniculaceum* (Nutt.) Coult. & Rose

56   *Cornus asperifolia* Michx.   Rough Dogwood
        = *C. drummondii* Meyer
56   *Uva-ursi uva-ursi* (L.) Britton   Bearberry
        = *Arctostaphylos uva-ursi* (L.) Spreng.
57   *Dasystephana puberula* (Michx.) Small   Gentian
        = *Gentiana puberulenta* Pringle
58   *Asclepias exaltata* (L.) Muhl.   Tall Milkweed
        = *A. viridiflora* Raf.
58   *Cuscuta paradoxa* Raf.   Dodder, Love Vine
        = *Cuscuta glomerata* Choisy
60   *Mentha canadensis* L.   Wild Mint
        = *M. arvensis* L.
61   *Agastache anethiodora* (Nutt.) Britton   Fragrant Giant Hyssop,
                                                         Wild Anise
        = *A. foeniculum* (Pursh) Kuntze
61   *Physalis lanceolata* Michx.   Prairie Ground Cherry
        = *P. longifolia* Nutt.
64   *Symphoricarpos symphoricarpos* (L.) MacM.   Coral Berry
        = *S. orbiculatus* Moench
64   *Pepo foetidissima* (H.B.K.) Britton   Wild Gourd
        = *Cucurbita foetidissima* H.B.K.
65   *Cucurbita lagenaria* L.   Dipper Gourd
        = *Lagenaria siceraria* (Molina) Standl.
65   *Pepo pepo* L.   Pumpkin
        = *Cucurbita pepo* L.
66   *Pepo maxima* (Duch.) Peterm.   Squash
        = *Cucurbita maxima* Duch.
68   *Citrullus citrullus* (L.) Karst.   Watermelon
        = *C. lanatus* (Thunb.) Mansf. (*C. vulgaris*)
77   *Micrampelis lobata* (Michx.) Greene   Wild Cucumber
        = *Echinocystis lobata* (Michx.) T. & G.
79   *Ratibida columnaris* (Sims) D. Don   Prairie Coneflower
        = *R. columnifera* (Nutt.) Woot. & Stanl.
80   *Ambrosia elatior* L.   Ragweed
        = *A. artemisiifolia* L.
80   *Boebera papposa* (Vent.) Rydb.   Fetid Marigold, Prairie-dog Food
        = *Dyssodia papposa* (Vent.) Hitchc.
81–82   *Lacinaria scariosa* (L.) Hill   Blazing Star
        = *Liatris aspera* Michx.
82   *Artemisia dracunculoides* Pursh   Fuzzy-weed
        = *A. dracunculus* L.
82   *Artemisia gnaphalodes* Nutt.   Wild Sage
        = *A. ludoviciana* Nutt.
Plate 17 *a,b* Apios tuberosa   Indian Potato
        = *Apios americana* Medic.

Errata

page

xvii   FOR 6. *a*. Erythronium mesochereum READ 6. *a*. Erythronium me-sochoreum

xvii   FOR 9. Irish versicolor READ 9. Iris versicolor

9   FOR *Pleurotus ulmarius* Bull. READ *Pleurotus ulmarius* (Bull. ex Fr.) Kummer

10   FOR *Morchella esculenta* (L.) Pers. READ *Morchella esculenta* L. ex Fr.

39   FOR *Thermopsis rhombifolia* (Nutt.) Richards READ *Thermopsis rhombifolia* Nutt. ex Richards

39   FOR *Melilotus alba* Desv. READ *Melilotus alba* Medic.

39   FOR *Melilotus officinalis* (L.) Lam. READ *Melilotus officinalis* (L.) Pall.

40   FOR *Glycyrhiza lepidota* Pursh. READ *Glycyrrhiza lepidota* Pursh.

60   FOR *Hedeoma hispida* Pursh. READ *Hedeoma hispidum* Pursh.

83   FOR *Arctium minus* Schk. READ *Arctium minus* Bernh.

84   FOR *Lygodesmia juncea* (Pursh) D. Don. READ *Lygodesmia juncea* (Pursh) Hook.

105   FOR Iris versicolor, 20 READ *Iris versicolor*, 20

106   FOR *Lepargyraea argentea*, 54 READ *Lepargyrea argentea*, 54

PREFACE

The results contained in the following paper are born of the desire to ascertain so far as possible the relation of the native people of the plains to one phase of their indigenous physical environment—its plant life—and their ingenuity in supplying their necessities and pleasures therefrom. It must be borne in mind that the sources of supply available to any of the tribes of the American race were greatly restricted as compared with the field from which our European race draws its supplies. Many of the plants of this continent utilized by its native people, however, might well be useful acquisitions for our people if made known to us.

Another potent reason for gathering such information while it may still be obtained, before the death of all the old people who alone possess it, is that it is only in the light of knowledge of physical environments that folklore, ritual, ceremony, custom, song, story, and philosophy can be interpreted intelligently. The intellectual and spiritual life of a people is reflected from their material life. The more fully and clearly the physical environment of a people is known the more accurately can all their cultural expressions be interpreted. The old people themselves appreciate this and have expressed themselves as glad to give me all the information they could in the matters of my inquiry, in order that, as they said, future generations of their own people as well as the white people may know and understand their manner of life. To this end my informants in the several tribes have taken pains and have shown great patience in instructing me in their lore.

The information here collated has been obtained at first hand from intelligent and credible old persons, thoroughly conversant with the matters which they discussed. The various items have been rigorously checked by independent corroborative evidence from other individuals of the same tribe and of different tribes through a protracted period. The work of the interpreters employed has also been verified by comparison and by my own study of the languages of the various tribes interviewed.

The information was obtained by bringing actual specimens of each plant to the observation and identification of many informants, and the names, uses, and preparation in each case were noted on the spot at the dictation of the informant.

I have met uniform courtesy, kindness, and hospitality at the hands of Indians of the several tribes in the pursuit of my inquiries, and my sincere thanks are due to very many men and women of the tribes, their great number preventing acknowledgment to them here by name. Special mention for conspicuous service rendered the author should be made of Dr. Susan La Flesche Picotte and her sister, Mrs. Walter T. Diddock, of Walthill, Nebr., daughters of Chief Iron Eye, otherwise Joseph La Flesche, of the Omaha tribe. Of the same tribe should be mentioned Wajapa, White Horse, George Miller, Daniel Webster, Amos Walker, and Richard Robinson.

Penishka, of the Ponca tribe, enrolled on the Government rolls as Jack Penishka, Niobrara, Nebr., has given much useful information of his tribe.

Of the Teton Dakota, mention should be made of Fast Horse and his wife, Joseph Horncloud, Otto Chiefeagle, and the well-known Short Bull.

Of the Pawnee, special thanks are due Mr. James R. Murie, Mr. Alfred Murie and his wife, Chief White Eagle, Mr. David Gillingham, Mrs. Rhoda Knife-Chief and Mr. Charles Knife-Chief.

My thanks are due also to Dr. Charles E. Bessey, of the University of Nebraska, for suggestions and encouragement in carrying on the work and to him and Mr. James Mooney for reading the manuscript.

I wish to acknowledge also my obligation to Mr. W. E. Safford for his painstaking aid in arranging and verifying the botanical nomenclature.

PHONETIC GUIDE

1. All vowels are to be given their continental values.

2. Superior n (^{n}) gives a nasal modification to the preceding vowel.

3. A consonant sound approximating the German *ch* is shown by *h*.

4. A lengthened vowel is shown by doubling, e.g. *buude, pakskiisu*, etc.

5. Unless indicated as a diphthong, vowels do not unite in sound, but each vowel forms a syllable.

USES OF PLANTS BY THE INDIANS OF THE MISSOURI RIVER REGION

By Melvin Randolph Gilmore

INTRODUCTION

During the period which has elapsed since the European occupancy of the continent of North America there has never been a thorough-going, comprehensive survey of the flora with respect to the knowledge of it and its uses possessed by the aboriginal population. Until recent years little study had been made of the ethnobotany of any of the tribes or of any phytogeographic region. Individual studies have been made, but the subject has not claimed a proportionate share of interest with other phases of botanical study. The people of the European race in coming into the New World have not really sought to make friends of the native population, or to make adequate use of the plants or the animals indigenous to this continent, but rather to exterminate everything found here and to supplant it with the plants and animals to which they were accustomed at home. It is quite natural that aliens should have a longing for the familiar things of home, but the surest road to contentment would be by way of gaining friendly acquaintance with the new environment. Whatever of good we may find in the new land need not exclude the good things we may bring from the old, but rather augment the sum total contributing to our welfare. Agriculture and horticulture should constantly improve the useful plants we already have, while discovery of others should be sought.

We shall make the best and most economical use of all our land when our population shall have become adjusted in habit to the natural conditions. The country can not be wholly made over and adjusted to a people of foreign habits and tastes. There are large tracts of land in America whose bounty is wasted because the plants which can be grown on them are not acceptable to our people. This is not because these plants are not in themselves useful and desirable, but because their valuable qualities are unknown. So long as the peo-

1

ple of the country do not demand articles of food other than those
to which our European ancestors were accustomed those articles will
be subject to demand in excess of production, with consequent en-
hancement of cost, while at the same time we have large land areas
practically unproductive because the plants they are best fitted to
produce are not utilized. The adjustment of American consumption
to American conditions of production will bring about greater im-
provement in conditions of life than any other material agency.
The people of any country must finally subsist on those articles of
food which their own soil is best fitted to produce. New articles of
diet must come into use, and all the resources of our own country
must be adequately developed.

Dr. J. W. Harshberger has well stated the practical uses and the
correlations of ethnobotanic study:

> Phytogeography, or plant geography in its widest sense, is concerned not
> only with the distribution of wild plants, but also with the laws governing the
> distribution of cultivated plants. In order to determine the origin of the lat-
> ter—that is, the original center from which the cultivation of such plants has
> spread—it is necessary to examine the historic, archeologic, philologic, eth-
> nologic, and botanic evidence of the past use of such plants by the aboriginal
> tribes of America. This investigation affords interesting data which can be
> applied practically in enlarging the list of plants adaptable to the uses of civi-
> lized man. . . . Ethnobotany is useful as suggesting new lines of modern
> manufacture, for example, new methods of weaving goods, as illustrated by
> the practical application of the careful studies of pueblo fabrics by Frank H.
> Cushing. It is of importance, therefore, to seek out these primitive races and
> ascertain the plants which they have found available in their economic life,
> in order that perchance the valuable properties they have utilized in their
> wild life may fill some vacant niche in our own, may prove of value in time
> of need or when the population of America becomes so dense as to require
> the utilization of all of our natural resources.[1]

NEGLECTED OPPORTUNITIES

That we have had in the past exceptional opportunities for obtaining aboriginal plant lore, which we have failed to recognize,
disdained to accept, or neglected to improve, is well shown by an
incident narrated in his journal by the great botanical explorer,
Bradbury, in the beginning of the nineteenth century. How much
information might then have been obtained which is no longer available! In 1809 Bradbury accompanied a trading expedition up the
Missouri River as far as the villages of the Arikara.

> I proceeded along the bluffs [in the vicinity of the Omaha village which was
> at that time near the place where Homer, Dakota County, Nebr., now is] and
> was very successful in my researches, but had not been long employed when
> I saw an old Indian galloping toward me. He came up and shook hands with

---

[1] Harshberger, Phytogeographic Influences in the Arts and Industries of American
Aborigines, p. 26.

me and, pointing to the plants I had collected, said, " Bon pour manger? " to which I replied, " Ne pas bon." He then said, " Bon pour medicine? " I replied, " Oui." He again shook hands and rode away. . . . On my return through the village I was stopped by a group of squaws, who invited me very kindly into their lodges, calling me *Wakendaga*[1] (physician). I declined accepting their invitation, showing them that the sun was near setting, and that it would be night before I could reach the boats. They then invited me to stay all night; this also I declined, but suffered them to examine my plants, for all of which I found they had names.[2]

ETHNIC BOTANY

In savage and barbarous life the occupation of first importance is the quest of food. In the earliest times people had to possess a practical working knowledge of plants with regard to their utilization for food; those which were edible, those by which shift could be made at need to avert famine, and those which on account of deleterious properties must be avoided at all times, came to be known by experience of all the people in their range.

In the process of experiment some plants would be found which, though not proving useful for food, would disclose properties which could be used as correctives of unhealthy conditions of the body; some would be found to allay fevers, some to stimulate certain functions, others having the effect to stop hemorrhage, and so on.

Certain persons in every tribe or social group, from taste and habit, would come to possess a fund of such knowledge, and to these all simpler folk, or those more occupied with other things, would resort. These wise ones then would know how to add the weight and dignity of ceremony and circumstance so that the laity should not fail to award due appreciation to the possessors of such knowledge; thus arose the rituals connected with the uses and the teaching of the same. Persons who desired to acquire such knowledge applied to those who possessed it, and if of approved character and prudence they, upon presentation of the customary fees or gifts, were duly instructed. These primitive professors of botany would then conduct their disciples on private excursions to the haunts of the plants and there impart to them the knowledge of the characteristics and habits, ecologic relations, and geographic distribution of the plants, together with their uses, methods, and time of gathering, preserving, and preparing for medicinal use, and the proper way to apply them.

---

[1] Bradbury must have been mistaken as to the meaning of the people or have misunderstood the term used, because the Omaha word for " physician " is *wazathe*. The word *wakaⁿdagi* means " something supernatural." This may be the word Bradbury heard and has given as *wakendaga*, or he may have misunderstood some other word No such word as *wakendaga* has been found by me in the Omaha language.

[2] Bradbury, Travels in the Interior of America, p. 75.

Besides this body of special plant lore there was also a great deal of knowledge of plants in general and their common uses, their range, habits, and habitat, diffused among the common people. There was also a body of folk sayings and myths alluding to plants commonly known.

INFLUENCE OF FLORA ON HUMAN ACTIVITIES AND CULTURE

The dominant character of the vegetation of a region is always an important factor in shaping the culture of that region, not only directly by the raw materials which it supplies or withholds, but indirectly also through the floral influence on the fauna. The chase of the buffalo with all that it entailed in habits of domestic life, instrumentalities and forms of government, industrial activities, and religious rites, was directly related to the prairie and plains formations of vegetation. The food staples, the style of housebuilding, and forms of industry were quite different in the prairie region from what they were in the eastern woodland regions, and in the desert region of the Southwest they were different from either of the first two regions.

The Dakota came into the prairie region from the east in the lake region, impelled by the onset of the Chippewa, who had the advantage of firearms acquired from the French. In the lake region they had as the most important article of vegetal food the grain of *Zizania aquatica*. As they migrated westward the quantity of *Zizania* diminished and the lack had to be supplied by substitution of something which the prairie might afford. One of the food plants of greatest importance they found on the prairie is *Psoralea esculenta*. The Dakota name of the wild rice, *Zizania aquatica*, is *psin* and of *Psoralea esculenta* is *tipsina*. From the etymology of these two names Dr. J. R. Walker, of Pine Ridge, has suggested that the second is derived from the first, indicating the thought of its usefulness as a food in place of what had been the plant of greatest importance in the food supply of the region formerly inhabited by this people. Doctor Walker offers this suggestion only as a possible explanation of the derivation of *tipsina*. *Tinta* is the Dakota word for "prairie"; *na* is a suffix diminutive. It is suggested, then, that in *tipsina* we have a compound from *tinta-psin-na*. This seems a plausible explanation. It need not imply that *Psoralea* was thought to be like *Zizania*, but only that it was a little plant of the prairie, *tinta*, which served a use like to that of *Zizania*, *psin*. This is probably a case in point, but whether so or not, instances could be cited of the influence of vegetation on language, as in case of some names of months, *Wazhushtecha-sha-wi*, Red Strawberry moon—i. e., the moon (lunar month) when strawberries are red ripe, the name of the month of June in the Dakota calendar.

The prevalence of certain plants often gave origin to place names. As examples of such names may be cited the Omaha name of Logan Creek, tributary of the Elkhorn River, *Taspaⁿ-hi-bate-ke* (meaning river where clumps of *Crataegus* are). Another instance is the Omaha name of Loup River, which is *Nu-taⁿ-ke* (river where *nu* abounds). *Nu* is the Omaha name of *Glycine apios*. The Omaha name of Little Blue River is *Maa-ozhi-ke* (river full of cottonwoods, *maa*).

The character of the flora of a region has its effect on the style of architecture. The tribes of the eastern woodlands had abundance of timber for building, so their houses were log structures or frames covered with bark. In Nebraska, where the forest growth was very limited, the dwelling was the earth lodge, a frame of timbers thatched with prairie grass and covered with earth.

A people living with nature, and largely dependent upon nature, will note with care every natural aspect in their environment. Accustomed to observe through the days and the seasons, in times of stress and of repose, every natural feature, they will watch for every sign of the impending mood of nature, every intimation of her favor and every monition of her austerity. Living thus in daily association with the natural features of a region some of the more notable will assume a sort of personality in the popular mind, and so come to have place in philosophic thought and religious ritual.

Throughout the range of the Plains tribes they saw everywhere the cottonwood, the willow, and the cedar. These trees by their appearance impressed the imagination of the primitive mind. The cedar; appearing to be withdrawn into lonely places, and standing dark and still, like an Indian with his robe drawn over his head in prayer and meditation, seemed to be in communion with the Higher Powers. The willow was always found along the watercourses, as though it had some duty or function in the world in connection with this element so imperatively and constantly needful to man and to all other living forms. The cottonwood they found in such diverse situations, appearing always so self-reliant, showing such prodigious fecundity, its lustrous young leaves in springtime by their sheen and by their restlessness reflecting the splendor of the sun like the dancing ripples of a lake, that to this tree also they ascribed mystery. This peculiarity of the foliage of the cottonwood is quite remarkable, so that it is said the air is never so still that there is not motion of cottonwood leaves. Even in still summer afternoons, and at night when all else was still, they could ever hear the rustling of cottonwood leaves by the passage of little vagrant currents of air. And the winds themselves were the paths of the Higher Powers, so they were constantly reminded of the mystic character of this tree.

The Sacred Pole, an object of the greatest veneration to the Omaha Nation, was made of cottonwood.

These three trees will serve as examples of plants to which mystery is ascribed and which had symbolism in the rituals of religion. In the chapter on the aboriginal uses of plants, where the plants are listed according to taxonomic order, several others will be found.

It will be found that the sense of beauty and the pleasure-giving arts will, with every people, find outlet and expression by means of the natural products of their own region. Much of the enjoyment of art arises from association. The tribes of Nebraska found within their range many plants yielding pigments to gratify the love of color; they also found many plants whose leaves or seeds yield fragrance. All of these scents are clean and wholesome and redolent of the pure outdoors and freshness of breezes from nature's garden and the farthest removed from any suggestion of hothouse culture and of the moiling of crowds. By a whiff of any of these odors one is mentally carried, by the power of association·and suggestion, to the wide, quiet spaces, where the mind may recover from throng-sickness and distraction of the multitude and regain power and poise.

Native plants of the region also furnished the materials for personal adornment, although it is noteworthy that it has not been found that flowers were used for this purpose by any of the tribes of the plains. It was often remarked that the people admired the wild flowers in their natural state, but they never plucked them. However, beads and pendants were made from many seeds.

INFLUENCE OF HUMAN POPULATION ON FLORA

It would be most interesting if we could determine with any degree of accuracy the efficient factors in the redistribution of vegetation over the ice-devastated region after the glacial retreat. We should like to know the distance, velocity, and direction, and the active agents, eolian, hydrographic, faunal, and anthropic, of the various currents in the resurgence of floral life over the region formerly ice covered.

We see the results of human agency as a factor in plant migration very clearly in the introduction into this State of a number of plants since the advent of Europeans. Some species introduced here are indigenous on the Atlantic seaboard, some have been brought from Europe and naturalized in the Eastern States, and thence brought here by immigrants from those States; other species, for instance *Salsola pestifer* (Russian thistle), have been introduced directly from Europe.

Verbascum thapsus (mullein), *Arctium minus* (burdock), *Leontodon taraxacum* (dandelion), and many other weeds now very common, are of recent introduction by this means, besides many plants purposely introduced by the white settlers, such as *Nepeta cataria* (catnip), *Roripa armoracia* (horseradish), and other herbaceous plants, and fruit and timber trees, vines, and shrubs.

Although these sources of plant immigration into Nebraska are recognized, the human factor in plant distribution prior to the European advent is not so obvious and may not have suggested itself to most of my readers. But the people of the resident tribes traveled extensively and received visitors from distant tribes. Their wants required for various purposes a great number of species of plants from mountain and plain and valley, from prairie and from woodland, from regions as remote from each other as the Rio Grande and the Great Lakes and St. Lawrence.

Their cultivated plants were all probably of Mexican origin, comprised in the *Cucurbitaceae* (squashes, pumpkins, gourds, and watermelons), *Phaseolus vulgaris* (garden bean) in 15 or more varieties, *Zea mays* (corn) in five general types aggregating from 15 to 20 varieties, and their tobacco, *Nicotiana quadrivalvis*.

But besides these known plant immigrants already carried into Nebraska by human agency before the advent of Europeans, certain facts lead me to believe that some plants not under cultivation, at least in the ordinary sense, owe their presence here to human transportation, either designed or undesigned. Parts of certain plants, and in most cases the fruits or fruiting parts, were desired and used for their fragrance, as the seeds of *Aquilegia canadensis*, the fruiting tops of *Thalictrum purpurascens*, the entire plant of *Galium triflorum*, the fruits of *Zanthoxylum americanum*, and leaves and tops of *Monarda fistulosa*. Any of these easily might be, and probably were, undesignedly distributed by the movements of persons carrying them. Desirable fruits were likely carried from camp to camp and their seeds dropped in a viable condition often in places favorable to their growth. *Malus ioensis* is found in Iowa and on the west side of the Missouri River in the southeast part of Nebraska, but nowhere higher up the Missouri on the west side except on a certain creek flowing into the Niobrara from the south near the line between Knox County and Holt County. The Omaha and Ponca call this creek Apple Creek on that account. The original seed, so far from their kind, probably reached this place in camp kitchen refuse.

Acorus calamus and *Lobelia cardinalis* are both found in certain restricted areas within the old Pawnee domain. *Acorus* is exceedingly highly prized by the Pawnee, and also by the other tribes, for medicinal use, and by the Pawnee especially for ritualistic religious use. Also its seeds were used for beads. Seeds obtained originally at a place far distant might have been lost in the margins of streams, and so have been introduced unwittingly. Moreover, seeds or living roots might have been brought purposely and set by the priests and doctors without the knowledge of the laity. Thus this plant may have been introduced to the few places where it is now to be found in Nebraska either with or without design. At all events it appears most probable that it was introduced by human agency. It is significant that the isolated areas where it is found are comparatively near old Pawnee village sites. *Lobelia* was a plant to which mystic power in love affairs was attributed. It was used in making love charms. Of course the methods and formulæ for compounding love medicines were not known to everyone, so a person desiring to employ such a charm must resort to some one reputed to have knowledge of it and must pay the fees and follow the instructions of his counsellor. In order to have the medicine convenient the wise ones might very naturally think of trying to introduce it to grow in their own country. Quite naturally, too, its introduction, if accomplished, would be secretly effected. Advertising is contrary to the professional code.

In another place the recent dissemination of *Melilotus* is discussed. When the Pawnee were removed from Nebraska to Oklahoma they carried with them seeds from Nebraska, their mother country, to the land, foreign to them, which circumstances they had no power to control caused them to colonize. Besides the seeds of their cultivated crops they carried stores of dried fruits as part of their food supply. Among these were quantities of dried plums, often dried entire without pitting. At the present time there are thickets of *Prunus americana* wherever are seen the lodge rings of the original earth lodges which they first occupied when they went to Oklahoma. This fact I observed when I visited that tribe in pursuit of information in their plant lore. From consideration of such facts as are here demonstrated I am of the opinion that human occupation and activities were more or less efficient factors in the distribution of plants in Nebraska as found by the first comers of the European race.

The most casual observer can perceive that Europeans, since their advent, have greatly changed the flora by introducing new species and depleting the numbers of some and augmenting the numbers of certain other species. A very great depletion has occurred in the grassland flora by reason of the large areas in which the original flora has been completely exterminated by the plow. Other areas have been overgrazed until the original balance of vegetation has been destroyed by the unnatural competition induced among the native species as well as by the added competitive factor of introduced species. Thus many pasture lands may now be seen in which hard and bitter species, such as *Solidago rigida* and *Vernonia fasciculata*, not desired by grazing animals, have inordinately increased. Not only have some species of the natural prairie flora been thus decreased and others increased, but the woodland flora has been considerably augmented not only by artificial planting, but also by attendant protection of the natural increase, which protection has been in some instances intentional and in others only coincidental.

The introduction and dissemination of species by human agency in aboriginal time has been discussed already. It remains to notice the human factor in depletion of certain species and augmentation of others prior to European advent. Probably the chief means employed by the tribes, affecting the floral balance, was that of fire. Their habit of firing the grasslands was effective in retarding the advance of woodland with all its associate flora and very probably even drove back the forest line and exterminated some areas which, previous to any human occupancy, had been possessed by forest growth.

TAXONOMIC LIST OF PLANTS USED BY INDIANS OF THE MISSOURI RIVER REGION [1]

PROTOPHYCEAE AND ZYGOPHYCEAE

Without specification of genera or even of orders it is sufficient to say that a green stain for decoration of implements made of wood was obtained from masses of the green aquatic vegetation popularly known as "pond scum" or "frog spit." The green substance used by the people of the tribes for the purpose of making a green stain, obtained by them from sluggish streams and ponds, doubtless consisted of colonies of *Protococcus*, *Ulothrix*, *Chaetophora*, *Spirogyra*, etc.

AGARICACEAE

PLEUROTUS ULMARIUS Bull. Elm Cap.

This fungus is used for food by the tribes acquainted with it. When young and tender it is most delicious. It grows in decayed spots on *Acer negundo* and *Ulmus* sp. The writer discovered its use for food among the people of the Dakota Nation. Some women were gathering it in a grove of boxelder near the place where the Cannonball River flows into the Missouri River, and they gave information

---

[1] See glossary of plant names, p. 139.

as to its use. They were looking for it in decayed spots caused by tapping the trees for the purpose of sugar making, for these people still make sugar from the sap of the boxelder.

POLYPORACEAE   BRACKET FUNGI

POLYSTICTUS VERSICOLOR (L.) Fr.

> *Chaⁿ naⁿkpa* (Dakota), "tree ears" (*chaⁿ*, wood or tree; *naⁿkpa*, ear).

The Dakota use this fungus for food when young and tender, except specimens growing on ash trees (*Fraxinus*), which they say are bitter. They are prepared by boiling.

USTILAGINACEAE   SMUTS

USTILAGO MAYDIS (DC.) Cda. Corn Smut.

> *Wahaba ǩthi* (Omaha-Ponca); literally, "corn sores" or "blisters" (*wahaba*, corn).

This fungus was used for food by both Omaha and Pawnee. For this purpose the spore fruits were gathered as soon as they appeared, while firm and white, and boiled. They were said to be very good.

LYCOPERDACEAE   PUFFBALLS

LYCOPERDON GEMMATUM Batsch., CALVATIA CYATHAFORMIS (Bosc.) Morg., BOVISTA PLUMBEA Pers. Puffball.

> *Hokshi chekpa* (Dakota), "baby's navel" (*hokshi*, baby; *chekpa*, navel).

The Pawnee name is *Kaho rahik* (*kaho*, the name + *rahik*, old), descriptive of it in the stage when it is used as a styptic.

The prairie mushrooms, commonly designated puffballs, were gathered and kept for use as a styptic for any wounds, especially for application to the umbilicus of newborn infants. From its universal application to this use among the Dakota is derived their name for the puffball. In the young stage it is used for food. It is used also as a styptic by the Ponca and the Omaha. While white and firm, before the spores formed, it was sometimes roasted for food by the Omaha, but this use was unknown to my informant among the Dakota.

HELVELLACEAE

MORCHELLA ESCULENTA (L.) Pers. Morel.

> *Mikai ǩthi* (Omaha-Ponca), "star sore" (*mikai*, star; *ǩthi*, sore).

They are much esteemed for food and are eaten boiled.

PARMELIACEAE

PARMELIA BORRERI Turn.   Lichen.
Cha^n wiziye (Dakota).

USNEACEAE

USNEA BARBATA Hoffm.   Lichen.
Cha^n wiziye (Dakota).
This lichen and the preceding one are by the Dakota used in the same way and given the same name. They were used to make a yellow dye for porcupine quills; for this purpose the lichens were boiled and the quills dipped in the resulting liquid.

EQUISETACEAE

EQUISETUM SP.   Horsetail, Scouring Rush, Snakegrass, Joint Rush.
Ma^{n}de idhe shnaha (Omaha-Ponca), "to-make-a-bow-smooth" (*ma^{n}de*, bow; *shnaha*, to smooth; *idhe* carries the idea of purpose or use). Designated also *shangga wathate* because horses (*shangga*) eat it with avidity.
Pakarut (Pawnee).
It was used by these tribes for polishing, as we use sandpaper. Winnebago children sometimes made whistles of the stems, but the older people warned them not to do so lest snakes should come.

PINACEAE   CONIFERS

PINUS MURRAYANA Oreg. Com.   Lodgepole Pine.
Wazi (Dakota).
While not indigenous to Nebraska, this tree was known and prized for use as tipi poles. The tribes of eastern Nebraska made trips to obtain it in its habitat or traded for it with their western neighbors.
JUNIPERUS VIRGINIANA L.   Cedar.
Hante or *ḣante sha* (Dakota); *sha*, "red."
Maazi (Omaha-Ponca).
Tawatsaako (Pawnee).
The fruits are known as *ḣante itika*, "cedar eggs." The fruits and leaves were boiled together and the decoction was used internally for coughs. It was given to horses also as a remedy for coughs. For a cold in the head twigs were burned and the smoke inhaled, the burning twigs and the head being enveloped in a blanket. Because the cedar tree is sacred to the mythical thunderbird, his nest being "in the cedar of the western mountains," cedar boughs were put on

the tipi poles to ward off lightning, "as white men put up lightning rods," my informant said.

In the year 1849–50 Asiatic cholera was epidemic among the Teton Dakota. The Oglala were encamped at that time where Pine Ridge Agency now is. Many of the people died and others scattered in a panic. Red Cloud, then a young man, tried various treatments, finally a decoction of cedar leaves. This was drunk and was used also for bathing, and is said to have proved a cure.

The Omaha-Ponca name for the cedar is *maazi*. Cedar twigs were used on the hot stones in the vapor bath, especially in purificatory rites. J. Owen Dorsey [1] says, "In the Osage traditions, cedar symbolizes the tree of life." Francis La Flesche [2] says:

> An ancient cedar pole was also in the keeping of the *We'zhiⁿshte* gens, and was lodged in the Tent of War. This venerable object was once the central figure in rites that have been lost. In creation myths the cedar is associated with the advent of the human race; other myths connect this tree with the thunder. The thunder birds were said to live "in a forest of cedars . . ." There is a tradition that in olden times, in the spring after the first thunder had sounded, in the ceremony which then took place this Cedar Pole was painted and anointed at the great tribal festival held while on the buffalo hunt.

As a remedy for nervousness and bad dreams the Pawnee used the smoke treatment, burning cedar twigs for the purpose.

Typhaceae

Typha latifolia L. Cat-tail. (Pl. 1, *b*.)

Wihuta-hu (Dakota); *wihuta*, "the bottom of a tipi" (*hu*, plant-body, herb, shrub, or tree; in a Dakota plant name *hu* signifies "plant," as does *hi* in the Omaha language).

Wahab' igaskonthe (Omaha-Ponca); *wahaba*, corn; *igaskonthe*, similar, referring to the appearance of the floral spikes synchronously with the maturing of the corn.

Ksho-hiⁿ (Winnebago); *ksho*, prairie chicken, *hiⁿ*, feather. The plucked down resembles in color and texture the finer feathers of the prairie chicken.

Hawahawa (Pawnee).

Kirit-tacharush (Pawnee), "eye itch" (*kirit*, eye; *tacharush*, itch); so named because the flying down causes itching of the eyes if it gets into them.

The down was used to make dressings for burns and scalds; on infants, to prevent chafing, as we use talcum; and as a filling for pillows and padding for cradle boards and in quilting baby wrappings. Pieces of the stem were essential elements in making the

---

[1] Siouan Cults, p. 391.
[2] Fletcher and La Flesche, The Omaha Tribe, pp. 457–458.

a. PULSATILLA PATENS. (PASQUE FLOWER)

b. TYPHA LATIFOLIA

Photo by courtesy of Public Museum of Milwaukee, Department of Education

a. SAGITTARIA LATIFOLIA

Photo by courtesy of Public Museum of Milwaukee, Department of
Education

b. A SLUGGISH STREAM GROWING FULL OF ARROWLEAF (SAGITTARIA LATIFOLIA)

ceremonial object of the Omaha and Ponca known as *niniba weawaṇ*, used in the Wawan ceremony. In a family in which the birth of a child was expected the women busied themselves in collecting a great quantity of the down of *Typha*, in a mass of which was laid the newborn infant; that which adhered after drying the mother removed by manipulation after moistening with milk from her breasts. Cotton fabrics were unknown to the Plains tribes previous to the coming of white traders, hence, instead of cotton diapers, pads of cat-tail down were used for the purpose by the mothers in these tribes.

ALISMACEAE

SAGITTARIA LATIFOLIA Willd. Arrowleaf. (Pl. 1A.)
   Pshitola (Dakota).
   Siⁿ (Omaha-Ponca).
   Siⁿ-poro (Winnebago).
   Kirit (Pawnee), " cricket " (from the likeness of the tuber to the
      form of a cricket) ; known also as *kits-kat*, " standing in water,"
      the tuber being termed *kirit*.

By all these tribes the tubers were used for food, prepared by boiling or roasting. The Pawnee must have some other use for the plant because an old medicine-man showed excited interest when he saw a specimen in my collection, but he did not communicate to me what the use is.

In the Omaha myth, " Ishtinike and the Four Creators," *Sagittaria* (*Siⁿ*) is mentioned,[1] also in the myth " How the Big Turtle Went to War."[2]

Peter Kalm[3] in 1749 mentions *Sagittaria* as a food plant among the Algonquian Indians:

> *Katniss* is another Indian name of a plant, the root of which they were likewise accustomed to eat, . . . It grows in low, muddy, and very wet ground. The root is oblong, commonly an inch and a half long, and one inch and a quarter broad in the middle; but some of the roots have been as big as a man's fists. The Indians either boiled this root or roasted it in hot ashes. . . . Their *katniss* is an arrow-head or *Sagittaria*, and is only a variety of the Swedish arrow-head or *Sagittaria sagittifolia*, for the plant above the ground is entirely the same, but the root under ground is much greater in the American than in the European. Mr. Osbeck, in his voyage to China, mentions that the Chinese plant a *Sagittaria*, and eat its roots. This seems undoubtedly to be a variety of this *katniss*.

---

[1] Dorsey, Ȼegiha Language, p. 554.
[2] Ibid, p. 256. (The translator mistranslated *siⁿ* " wild rice." *Siⁿ* is *Sagittaria ;* wild rice is *Siⁿ waninde.*)
[3] Peter Kalm. Travels into North America, vol. I, p. 386.

POACEAE

SPARTINA MICHAUXIANA Hitchc. Slough Grass.

Sidu-hi (Omaha-Ponca).

This plant, which grows in all the swales of eastern Nebraska, was used as thatching to support the earth covering of the lodges in the permanent villages.

SAVASTANA ODORATA (L.) Scribn. Sweet Grass.

Wachanga (Dakota.)

Pezhe zonsta (Omaha-Ponca).

Manuska (Winnebago).

Kataaru (Pawnee).

Sweet grass is found in northeastern Nebraska, and more abundantly northward and eastward. It was used for perfume and was burned as an incense in any ceremony or ritual to induce the presence of good influences or benevolent powers, while wild sage, a species of *Artemisia*, was burned to exorcise evil influences or malevolent powers. It was an essential element in the objects used in the Wawan ceremony of the Omaha and Ponca. According to J. Owen Dorsey, *wachanga* is one of the plants used in connection with the sun dance.[1]

On Palm Sundays old Dakotas, members of the church, when they have received palms at the church, carry them home and tie sweet grass with them when they put them up in their houses. At the present time, it is said, some of the old people still carry sweet grass to church for the Palm Sunday service. This is from the old-time association of sweet grass with sacred ceremonies and things holy.

When Chief Welkie, of the Pembina band of the Chippewa tribe, made a treaty of peace with the Dakota tribe the ceremony included the smoking of a pipe of tobacco mixed with sweet grass. This was, no doubt, with the idea of summoning all good powers as witnesses and helpers in concluding the desired peace.

PANICUM VIRGATUM L. Switch Grass.

Hade wathazhninde (Ponca).

On the buffalo hunt, in cutting up the meat the people were careful to avoid laying it on grass of this species in head, because the glumes of the spikelets would adhere to the meat and afterwards would stick in the throat of one eating it.

STIPA SPARTEA Trin. Porcupine Grass, Spanish Needles, Needle Grass. (Pl. 2.)

Mika-hi (Omaha-Ponca), " comb plant " (*mika*, comb).

Pitsuts (Pawnee), " hairbrush "; or *Paari pitsuts*, Pawnee hairbrush.

---

[1] Siouan Cults, p. 454.

a. A MASS OF STIPA SPARTEA BENT UNDER THE WIND. IN THE BACKGROUND CAN BE SEEN A NUMBER OF PLANTS OF ECHINACEA ANGUSTIFOLIA IN BLOOM

b. BUNCH OF STIPA SPARTEA; BUNCH OF LONG-AWNED SEEDS OF STIPA SPARTEA; A HAIR-BRUSH MADE FROM AWNS OF STIPA SPARTEA

Photos by courtesy of Department of Botany, Iowa State Agricultural College

a. ZIZANIA AQUATICA (WILD RICE). HERBARIUM SPECIMEN OF STRAW, A FEW GRAINS NOT HULLED, AND A HANDFUL OF HULLED GRAINS AS PREPARED FOR FOOD

b. ZIZANIA AQUATICA, HABIT

Photo by courtesy of Public Museum of Milwaukee, Department of Education

The stiff awns of this grass were firmly bound into a bundle, from which the pointed grains were burned off, leaving a brush used for dressing the hair. This brush was used also in a certain part of the ceremony heretofore mentioned as the Wawan of the Omaha-Ponca, the Hako [1] of the Pawnee.

ZIZANIA AQUATICA L. Wild Rice, Indian Rice. (Pl. 3.)
Psiⁿ (Dakota).
Siⁿwaninda (Omaha-Ponca).
Siⁿ (Winnebago).

The range of wild rice is very extensive throughout the North Temperate Zone. It is found in the shallow lakes of the Sand Hills of Nebraska, still more northeastward in the lake region of Minnesota, Wisconsin, and Michigan, and northward into Canada. This cereal was an important part of the dietary of the tribes of Nebraska, but not in so great a degree as with the tribes of the lake regions toward the northeast. It would seem worth while to raise wild rice in any lakes and marshy flood plains in our State not otherwise productive, and so add to our food resources. From trial I can say that it is very palatable and nutritious and, to my taste, the most desirable cereal we have. A quotation from a consular report characterizes it as " the most nutritious cereal in America." [2] The most exhaustive treatise on wild rice and its use among the aboriginal tribes is that by Dr. A. E. Jenks. [3]

ZEA MAYS L. Maize, Indian Corn.
Wamnáheza (Dakota) ; Teton dialect, *wagmeza.*
Wahába (Omaha-Ponca).
Nikíís (Pawnee).

Maize was cultivated by all the tribes of Nebraska. Native informants say they had all the general types—dent corn, flint corn, flour corn, sweet corn, and pop corn; and that of most of these types they had several varieties. They maintained the purity of these varieties from generation to generation by selecting typical ears for seed and by planting varieties at some distance from each other. They raised considerable quantities, part of which was preserved by drying in the green stage, while the rest was allowed to ripen. The ripe corn was prepared by pounding to a meal, by parching (sometimes by parching and then grinding), by hulling with lye from ashes to make hominy, and in various other ways. Maize comprised a large part of the food supply. Corn was regarded as " mother " among the Nebraska tribes who cultivated it.

---

[1] Fletcher, The Hako, p. 220.
[2] *Outlook*, May 10, 1913, p. 80.
[3] The Wild Rice Gatherers of the Upper Lakes, in *Nineteenth Rep. Bur. Amer. Ethn.*, pt. 2.

When the corn was approaching maturity, an¹ blackbirds made depredations on the fields, the men of the Wazhinga-thatazhi subgens of the Omaha tribe used to chew up some grains of corn and spit the chewed corn around over the field. This action was supposed to keep the birds from doing any further damage.[1]

In the Omaha subgens, the Wazhinga-thatazhi ("those who eat no small birds"), the people feared to eat the first mature ears lest the small birds, particularly blackbirds, should come and devour the rest of the crop.[2]

A white leaf appearing in a cornfield was hailed with joy by the Omaha as a portent of a bountiful crop for the year and of abundance of meat at the next buffalo hunt.

Among the Omaha if a murderer passed near a field it was feared the effect would be to blight the crop. Some time in the latter half of the nineteenth century a murderer, having passed his term of exile for his crime, was returning to his people. As he approached he was warned away from the fields by their owners. This individual was a mystery man (" medicine man ") and as such was considered to possess supernatural power, or to be able to enlist the aid of supernatural powers by certain prayers and songs; hence as he came by the fields he sang a song to the powers to avert the disastrous effect on the crop, which otherwise his presence might incur. Of this he assured the people to quiet their fears of blight on their crop.

Corn silks were gathered and, after being dried in the sun, were stored away for use as food. To this end the dried corn silks were ground with parched corn, and, it is said, gave sweetness to the compound.

Our European race little appreciates the great number and variety of corn food products made by the American tribes. No attempt is here made even to give a full list of such products.

ANDROPOGON FURCATUS Muhl.

Ḣade-zhide (Omaha-Ponca), "red hay" (*ḣade*, hay; *zhide*, red).

This grass, the most common in the meadows and prairies of the State, was ordinarily used to lay on the poles to support the earth covering of the lodges. The stiff, jointed stems are termed in the Omaha-Ponca language *peska*. These were often used by little boys in play to make arrows for their toy bows. In making arrows of the stems of this wild grass small boys of the Arikara, Mandan, and Hidatsa tribes would commonly inse'rt a thorn of *Crataegus* sp. (thorn apple) for an arrow point. With such arrows to their little bows they would train themselves to skill in archery by shooting frogs. The first field matron to the Omaha taught the women to knit. One woman, Ponka-saⁿ, lost her needles and improvised a set from

---

[1] Dorsey, Omaha Sociology, p. 238.
[2] Dorsey, Siouan Cults, p. 402.

peska. White Horse, an old medicine-man of the Omaha, told me of a remedial use of *Andropogon* which he had obtained by purchase from an Oto medicine-man. A decoction of the lower blades of this grass chopped fine was drunk in cases of general debility and languor without definitely known cause. The same decoction was used also for bathing in case of fevers, for this purpose a cut being made on the top of the head to which the decoction was applied. The people had great dread of fevers because of the evil effect they were supposed to have on the mind; this no doubt was because of delirium which often accompanies fever.

CYPERACEAE

SCIRPUS VALIDUS Vahl. Bulrush.

Psa (Dakota).

Sa-hi (Omaha-Ponca).

Sistat (Pawnee).

The tender white part at the base of the stem of the bulrush was eaten fresh and raw by the Dakota. The stems were used to weave into matting by all the tribes. A medicine-man of the Pawnee evinced lively interest when he saw a specimen in my collection, but did not communicate any information about it, a fact from which I infer it has some ceremonial use.

ARACEAE

ARISAEMA TRIPHYLLUM (L.) Torr. Jack-in-the-pulpit. (Pl. 4.)

Mikasi-maka^n (Omaha-Ponca), "coyote medicine."

Nikso kororik kahtsu nitawau (Pawnee); medicine (or herb) *kahtsu;* that bears, *nitawau;* what resembles, *kororik;* an ear of corn, *nikso.* The name is strikingly descriptive of the ripened fruit.

This plant is used medicinally by the Pawnee. When a Pawnee medicine-man saw my specimen he evinced lively interest and showed me a bag containing the pulverized corm, but was unwilling to tell me its use. Another Pawnee medicine-man, however, told me of its use in treating headache by dusting on the top of the head and on the temples.

The corm was pulverized and applied as a counterirritant for rheumatism and similar pains, as irritant plasters are used by white people.

The seeds of this plant were put into gourd shells by the Pawnee to make rattles.

ACORUS CALAMUS L. Sweet Flag, Calamus.

Si^{n}kpe-ta-wote (Dakota), "muskrat food" (*si^{n}kpe*, muskrat; *wote*, food).

Makaⁿ-ninida (Omaha-Ponca).

Maⁿkaⁿ-kereḱ (Winnebago).

Kahtsha itu (Pawnee) ; *kahtsu*, medicine; *ha*, in water; *itu*, lying.

All the tribes hold this plant in very high esteem. It was used as a carminative, a decoction was drunk for fever, and the rootstock was chewed as a cough remedy and as a remedy for toothache. For colic an infusion of the pounded root stock was drunk. As a remedy for colds the rootstock was chewed or a decoction was drunk, or it was used in the smoke treatment. In fact, this part of the plant seems to have been regarded as a panacea. When a hunting party came to a place where the calamus grew the young men gathered the green blades and braided them into garlands, which they wore round the neck for their pleasant odor. It was one of the plants to which mystic powers were ascribed. The blades were used also ceremonially for garlands. In the mystery ceremonies of the Pawnee are songs about the calamus.

Among the Teton Dakota in old times warriors chewed the rootstock to a paste, which they rubbed on the face to prevent excitement and fear in the presence of the enemy.

COMMELINACEAE

TRADESCANTIA VIRGINICA L. Spiderwort, Spider Lily. (Pl. 5, *a*.)

This is a charmingly beautiful and delicate flower, deep blue in color, with a tender-bodied plant of graceful lines. There is no more appealingly beautiful flower on the western prairies than this one when it is sparkling with dewdrops in the light of the first beams of the rising sun. There is about it a suggestion of purity, freshness, and daintiness.

When a young man of the Dakota Nation is in love, and walking alone on the prairie he finds this flower blooming, he sings to it a song in which he personifies it with the qualities of his sweetheart's character as they are called to his mind by the characteristics figuratively displayed by the flower before him. In his mind the beauties of the flower and of the girl are mutually transmuted and flow together into one image.

The following song, addressed to *Tradescantia*, is translated from the Dakota language by Dr. A. McG. Beede:

> " Wee little dewy flower,
> So blessed and so shy,
> Thou'rt dear to me, and for
> My love for thee I'd die."

a. ARISAEMA TRIPHYLLUM

Photo by courtesy of Public Museum of Milwaukee, Department of Education

b. HABIT PICTURE OF ARISAEMA TRIPHYLLUM. PANAX TRIFOLIUM MAY ALSO BE SEEN

Photo by George R. Fox, Appleton, Wis.

a. TRADESCANTIA VIRGINICA (SPIDERWORT)

b. A CIRCLE OF COTTONWOOD-LEAF TOY TIPIS AS MADE BY INDIAN CHILDREN
OF PLAINS TRIBES

a. ERYTHRONIUM MESOCHOREUM, ENTIRE PLANT,
BULBS, AND FLOWERS

b. ERYTHRONIUM MESOCHOREUM, HABIT OF GROWTH ON THE
PRAIRIE

Photos by courtesy of Dr. Elda Walker, University of Nebraska

a. YUCCA GLAUCA IN BLOOM

Photo by courtesy of Dr. R. J. Pool, University of Nebraska

b. YUCCA GLAUCA IN FRUIT

a   b   c

a. A BUNDLE OF YUCCA LEAVES BOUND UP TO DEMONSTRATE USE AS DRILL IN FIRE MAKING.
b. A PIECE OF YUCCA STEM PREPARED TO DEMONSTRATE USE AS HEARTH PIECE IN FIRE
MAKING. c. A DRY YUCCA PLANT

LILIACEAE

ALLIUM MUTABILE Michx. Wild Onion.
Pshi^n (Dakota).
Ma^nzho^nka-mantanaha (Omaha-Ponca).
Shi^nhop (Winnebago).
Osidiwa (Pawnee).

Since the introduction of the cultivated onion the wild onion is known to the Pawnee as *Osidiwa tsitschiks*, " native *osidiwa*."

All the species of wild onion found within their habitat were used for food by the Nebraska tribes, commonly raw and fresh as a relish, sometimes cooked as a flavor for meat and soup, also fried.

ERYTHRONIUM MESOCHOREUM Knerr and E. ALBIDUM Nutt. Spring
    Lily, Snake Lily. (Pl. 6.)
Hedte-shutsh (Winnebago).

I was informed by Winnebago that children ate them raw with avidity when freshly dug in springtime.

LILIUM UMBELLATUM Pursh.

The flowers of this plant, pulverized or chewed, were applied by the Dakota as an antidote for the bites of a certain small poisonous brown spider. It is said to relieve the inflammation and swelling immediately.

YUCCA GLAUCA Nutt. Soapweed, Spanish Bayonet, Dagger Weed.
    (Pls. 7, 8.)
Hupestula (Dakota).
Duwaduwa-hi (Omaha-Ponca).
Chakida-kahtsu or *Chakila-kahtsu* (Pawnee).

The root was used by the Pawnee and Omaha in the smoke treatment. By all the tribes the root was used like soap, especially for washing the hair. On the high treeless plains the Teton Dakota, for want of wood for fire-drills, utilized yucca. The hard, sharp-pointed blades were bound together with sinew to make the drill, and the stem, peeled and dried, was used as the hearth of the fire-making apparatus, just as punk was used in the timbered regions.

Yucca leaves were macerated till the fibers were cleared, and, with the sharp, hard point of the leaf still attached, were twined into thread. The sharp point was used as a needle.

SMILAX HERBACEA L. Jacob's Ladder.
Toshunuk akunshke (Winnebago), " otter armlet " (*toshunuk.*
    otter; *akunshke*, armlet).

The fruits were eaten at times by the Omaha for their pleasant taste. They were said to be effectual in relieving hoarseness.

IRIDACEAE

IRIS VERSICOLOR L.   Blue Flag.   (Pl. 9.)

Makaⁿ-skithe [1] (Omaha-Ponca), " sweet medicine " (makaⁿ, medicine; skithe, sweet), or perhaps in this case meaning not " sweet "
in the sense we use the word, but " stimulating," as the plant has
a pungent taste.

The rootstock was pulverized and mixed with water, or more often
with saliva, and the infusion dropped into the ear to cure earache;
it was used also to medicate eye-water.   A paste was made to apply
to sores and bruises.

SALICACEAE

POPULUS SARGENTII Dode.   Cottonwood.   (Pl. 5, b.)

Wága chaⁿ (Dakota); chaⁿ means " wood " or " tree."

Maa zhoⁿ (Omaha-Ponca), " cotton tree " (zhoⁿ, wood or tree).

Natakaaru (Pawnee).

The Teton Dakota say that formerly the people peeled the young
sprouts and ate the inner bark because of its pleasant, sweet taste
and nutritive value.   Young cottonwood branches and upper branches
of older trees were provided as forage for their horses and were
said to be as " good for them as oats."   White trappers and travel-
ers have recorded their observations as to the value of the cottonwood as forage.

Mystic properties were ascribed to the cottonwood.   The Sacred
Pole of the Omaha was made from a cottonwood.   This was an object
which seems to have had among that people a function somewhat
similar to that of the Ark of the Covenant among the ancient He-
brews.   Among the list of personal names pertaining to the Kaⁿza
gens of the Omaha tribe is that of Maa-zhoⁿ Ḣoda, Gray Cottonwood.   Cottonwood bark was employed as a fuel for roasting the
clays used in making paints for heraldic and symbolic painting of
the skin.   A yellow dye was made from the leaf buds in early spring.
A very pretty and interesting use of cottonwood leaves was made by
children in play.   They split a leaf a short distance down from the
tip along the midrib; at equal distances from the tip they tore across
from the margin slightly; then, bending back the margin above the
rents for the smoke flaps, and drawing together the leaf-margins
below the rents and fastening them with a splinter or a thorn, they
had a toy tipi.   These they made in numbers and placed them in
circles like the camp circle of their tribe.   The children of all the
Nebraska tribes played thus.   It is interesting to note this manifesta-

---

[1] It should be noted that a number of different plants seem to be known by the
Omaha and Ponka as makaⁿ–skithe, " sweet medicine."

IRIS VERSICOLOR

Photo by courtesy of George R. Fox, Appleton, Wis.

tion of the inventive genius and resourcefulness of the Indian child mind thus reacting to its environment and providing its own amusement. Children sometimes gathered the cottony fruits of the cottonwood before they were scattered by the wind and used them as gum for chewing. In early spring, before the leaves appear, the waxy buds of the cottonwood were boiled to make yellow dye. Feathers for pluming arrows were dyed a yellowish color by dipping in a decoction made by boiling the seed vessels of this tree.

Mention has been made already of the use of cottonwood leaves by little girls in making toy tipis. They were also used to make toy moccasins. For this purpose a rent was made at equal distances on each side of the leaf about halfway from the tip to the petiole. The edge of the leaf was now turned down in a line from this rent to the base; then the edges of the leaf from the rent to the tip were brought together and pinned with a splinter to make the fore part, the edges of the base were brought together and fastened to make the back part, and behold! a tiny green moccasin of the pattern common among the tribes of the plains, the top being turned down at the ankle.

Girls and young women made another pleasing use of the cottonwood leaf. The tip of the leaf was put between the lips and the sides pressed against the nostrils with the thumb and index finger in such a way that one nostril was quite closed and the other partly so. Then the breath was expelled through the partly closed nostril, vibrating on the leaf in such a way that very sweet musical notes were produced, birdlike or flutelike in quality. The effect is most pleasing to the ear.

The green, unopened fruits of cottonwood were used by children as beads and ear pendants in play.

SALIX INTERIOR Rowlee. Sandbar Willow.

The stems of this willow were peeled and used in basketry by the Omaha and other tribes.

SALIX SP.

Wakpe-popa (Dakota), generic name for willow.

Ruhi (Winnebago).

Kitapato (Pawnee).

Poles of willow of various species, overlaid on the heavier timbers to sustain the thatch covered with earth, were used in the construction of the earth lodge. Small poles of willow were used to form the frame of the sudatory, or bath lodge. Before European customs had so far superseded the native tribal customs, willow had its place in the funeral customs of the Omaha. On the day of burial, the fourth day after the death, at the time of starting from the home for the place of interment, young men, friends of the family of the deceased, appeared at the lodge to accompany the funeral party to the grave. They made parallel gashes in the skin of the forearm, and lifting the skin between these gashes, they thrust in the stems of willow twigs; leaving these thus depending from the arm, the twigs were soon bathed in the blood of the young men, who thus attested to the living their sympathy and condolence, while they sang the tribal Song to the Spirit. This song is one of joyful cadence rather than mournful, because it is a song of cheer to the departing spirit, while their blood and tears manifest their sympathetic feeling for the bereaved

JUGLANDACEAE

JUGLANS NIGRA L. Black Walnut.

Hma (Dakota); Teton dialect, *gma;* also by the Teton Dakota called *cha^n-sapa*, black wood.

Tdage (Omaha-Ponca). *Tdage-hi*, walnut tree.

Chak (Winnebago). *Chak-hu*, walnut tree.

Sahtaku (Pawnee).

The nuts were used for food and a black dye was made from the root. The black walnut (*tdage*) is mentioned in the myth of "Ishtinike and the Four Creators."[1] For food the nuts were eaten plain or served with honey, or made into soup.

HICORIA OVATA (Mill.) Britton. Hickory Nut.

Cha^nsu (Dakota). *Cha^nsu-hu*, hickory tree.

No^nsi (Omaha-Ponca). *No^nsi-hi*, hickory tree.

Pa^nja (Winnebago), nut. *Pa^nja-hu*, nut tree.

Sahpakskiisu (Pawnee), skull nut, from the resemblance of the nut (*saht*, nut; *pakskiisu*, skull).

The nuts were used for food in the same way as walnuts. Sugar was made from the sap as from *Acer* species, and also by boiling hickory chips.

BETULACEAE

CORYLUS AMERICANA Walt. Hazelnut.

Uma (Dakota). *Uma-hu*, hazel bush.

U^nzhinga (Omaha-Ponca). *U^nzhinga-hi*, hazel bush.

Huksik (Winnebago).

The nuts were used for food as were other nuts, being eaten raw with honey, or used as body for soup.

---

[1] Dorsey, Ȼegiha Language, p. 556.

BETULA PAPYRIFERA Marsh. Paper or Canoe Birch.

Ta^npa (Dakota). *Ta^npa-hu*, birch tree. Teton dialect *Cha^nha sa^n*, pale-bark (*cha^n-ha*, bark; *sa^n* pale).

The bark, shredded fine, was bound in bundles for torches. It was used also as material for vessels to catch the sap from the trees in sugar-making time, and for various household utensils.

FAGACEAE

QUERCUS MACROCARPA Michx. Bur Oak.

Uskuyecha-hu (Dakota).
Tashka-hi (Omaha-Ponca).
Chashke-hu (Winnebago).
Patki-natawawi (Pawnee); *patki*, acorn; *natawawi*, bearing.

QUERCUS RUBRA L. Red Oak.

Uta (Dakota). *Uta-hu*, oak tree.
Buude-hi (Omaha-Ponca).
Nahata-pahat (Pawnee), " red-tree " (*nahata*, tree; *pahat*, red).

Acorns, especially of *Quercus rubra*, were used for food. The bitter and astringent properties were extracted by leaching with wood ashes, preferably the ashes from basswood. The bark of the root of any species of oak was scraped off and boiled and the decoction given for bowel trouble, especially in children.

ULMACEAE

ULMUS AMERICANA L. White Elm, American Elm.

Pe (Dakota), " the elm "; *pe cha^n*, " elm wood "; *pe ikcheka*, " the common elm."
Ezho^n zho^n (Omaha-Ponca), " elm tree," generic name; *ezho^n zho^n ska*, " white elm " (*ska*, white).
Taitsako taka (Pawnee), " white elm " (*taitsako*, elm: *taka*. white).

The wood was used for fuel; forked trees were used for the posts in building the earth lodge: sections of elm logs were used to make huge corn mortars, while the pestles were also made of this wood. Smaller mortars and pestles of this wood were made for grinding medicines and perfumes. All these uses applied also to the other species of elm.

ULMUS THOMASI Sarg. Rock Elm.

Pe itazipa (Dakota), " bow elm " (*itazipa*, bow).
Ezho^n zho^n zi (Omaha-Ponca), " yellow elm " (*zi*, yellow).

This species and the preceding were both used for saddle trees. It would seem from the Dakota name that it was formerly used for making bows, but I have no direct information on that point.

ULMUS FULVA Michx. Slippery Elm or Red Elm.

Pe tututupa (Dakota), or in Teton dialect *pe tutu*ⁿ*tu* ⁿ*pa.*

*Ezho*ⁿ *zhide* (Omaha-Ponca), " red elm " (*zhide*, red) or *ezho*ⁿ *zhide gthigthide*, " slippery red elm " (*gthigthide*, slippery).

Wakidikidik (Winnebago).

Taitsako pahat (Pawnee), " red elm " (*pahat*, red).

The bark, when weathered for several years till it glows with phosphorescence in the darkness, was used to catch the spark in fire-making. The fresh inner bark was boiled and the resulting decoction was drunk as a laxative. The Omaha used to cook the inner bark with buffalo fat in rendering out the tallow. They considered that the bark gave a desirable flavor to the fat and added a preservative quality, preventing it from becoming rancid. When the rendering was finished the children always asked for the pieces of cooked bark, which they prized as titbits.

The inner bark fiber was also used for making ropes and cords.

CELTIS OCCIDENTALIS L. Hackberry.

Yamnumnugapi (Dakota), from *yamnumnuga*, " to crunch," because animals crunch its berries.

Gube (Omaha-Ponca).

Wake-warutsh (Winnebago), " raccoon food " (*wake*, raccoon; *warutsh*, food).

Kaapsit (Pawnee).

Omaha informants say the berries were eaten only casually, but the Dakota used them as a flavor for meat. For this purpose they pounded them fine, seeds and all. When they first saw pepper corns of black pepper, and their use as a condiment when ground, they likened them to *yamnumnugapi* and so they called black pepper *yamnumnugapi washichu*ⁿ, "white man's *yamnumnugapi.*"

The Pawnee say they pounded the berries fine, added a little fat, and mixed them with parched corn. They described the combination as very good.

MORACEAE

TOXYLON POMIFERUM Raf. Osage Orange, Bois d'Arc.

*Zho*ⁿ*-zi-zhu* (Omaha-Ponca), " yellow-flesh wood " (*zho*ⁿ, wood; *zi*, yellow; *zhu*, flesh).

Nakitsku (Pawnee).

This tree was not native to Nebraska, but its wood was used for making bows whenever it could be obtained. It was gotten whenever southern trips were made into its range, which is in the southern part of Oklahoma; or it was obtained by gift or barter from the tribes of that region.

HUMULUS AMERICANA Nutt. Hops.

Chaⁿ iyuwe (Dakota), but this only means twining, *iyuwe*, on a tree, *chaⁿ*. Since its European use in connection with yeast has become known to them they call it *wahpe onapohye; wahpe*, "leaves"; *onapohye*, "to puff up."

Makaⁿ skithe (Omaha-Ponca), "sweet medicine." Since learning its leavening use it is called in that connection *wiunabiku*.

The Teton Dakota steeped the fruits to make a drink to allay fevers and intestinal pains. A part of the root down 3 or 4 feet in the ground was called *makaⁿ skithe*, "sweet medicine"; this was chewed and applied to wounds, either alone or in combination with the root of *Physalis lanceolata*, "the crooked medicine," and that of *Anemone canadensis*, "the little buffalo medicine."

URTICACEAE

URTICA GRACILIS Ait. Nettle.

Hanuga-hi or *manazhiha-hi* (Omaha-Ponca).

The dried stalks were crumpled in the hands or gently pounded with a stone to free the fiber from the woody part. The first method was more common. The fiber of nettles was used by Nebraska tribes for spinning twine and cordage. Rope of this fiber was generally used to hobble horses. It was also used to weave into cloth. It is said that cloth of this fiber was used in the Sacred Bundle of the Tent of War.

Small boys gathered the fiber of this plant to use as wadding for their popguns.

POLYGONACEAE

RUMEX CRISPUS L. Sour Dock.

Shiakipi (Dakota).

Among the Teton Dakota the green leaves, crushed, were bound on boils to draw out the suppuration. The Omaha boiled the leaves for food as white people do. This plant is naturalized from Europe.

RUMEX HYMENOSEPALUS Torr. Canaigre.

Kahts-pirakari or *kahts-pilakari* (Pawnee), "medicine with many children" (*kahtsu*, medicine; *pira* or *pila*, children; *kari*, many), so called because of the sweet-potato-like roots clustered at the base of the stem.

The plant is found indigenous in sandy slopes of river valleys in the region of the Wichita Mountains of Oklahoma and southwestward. Since the allotment of their lands in severalty, the Wichita and Pawnee are bringing this plant into cultivation. The root is used as a remedy for diarrhea.

CHENOPODIACEAE

CHENOPODIUM ALBUM L.   Lamb's-quarter.

Walpe toto (Dakota), " greens " (*walpe*, leaves; *toto*, green).

Kitsarius (Pawnee), " green juice " (*kits*, from *kitsu*, water, juice; *kidarius*, green).

This plant is naturalized from Europe, but appears to be so long established that the fact of its introduction seems now unknown to the Indians.   Among the Teton Dakota and the Omaha this plant, while young and tender, was cooked as pottage.   A Pawnee informant said that it is so used now by the Pawnee, not in former times.   It was used in old times by the Pawnee for painting bows and arrows green.

NYCTAGINACEAE

ALLIONIA NYCTAGINEA Michx.   Wild Four-o'clock.

Poípie (Dakota).

Makaⁿ-wasek (Omaha-Ponca), " strong medicine " (*makaⁿ*, medicine; *wasek*, strong).

Kahtstakat (Pawnee), " yellow medicine " (*kahts*, from *kahtsu*, medicine; *takat*, yellow).

By the Teton Dakota the root was boiled to make a decoction to drink in case of fever.   Together with roots of *Echinacea angustifolia* it was boiled to make a vermifuge.   The prescription for this purpose required the drinking of it four nights at bedtime, after which, at the next evacuation, the worms would be voided.   My informant, Fast Horse, of the Oglala tribe, said, " If one has a big worm [tape worm?], it comes away, too."   Roots of *Allionia* and *Echinacea* were also boiled together to make a remedy for swellings of arms or legs.   When applied, this must always be rubbed downward on the affected parts to reduce the swelling.   Among the Ponka the root was used as a remedy for wounds, for this purpose being chewed and blown into them.   Among the Pawnee the dried root, ground fine, was applied dry as a remedy for sore mouth in babies. A decoction of the root was drunk by women after childbirth to reduce abdominal swelling.

PHYTOLACCACEAE

PHYTOLACCA AMERICANA L.   Pokeberry, Inkberry, Redweed.

The plant seems to be unknown to the Omaha, Ponca, and Dakota, and known only in recent times to the Oto and Pawnee.   It is a late introduction from the Eastern States and is reported only from the extreme southeastern part of the State.   It is rather common in Oklahoma, whither the Oto, the Pawnee, and most of the Ponca have been removed.   So far as I was able to learn, they have there used it only for decorative purposes, a red stain obtained from the fruit being employed in painting horses and various articles of use or adornment.

NYMPHAEACEAE

NYMPHAEA ADVENA Soland. Large Yellow Pond Lily.

There is some dialectic variation in the speech of the four tribes of the Pawnee Nation, and by one tribe, the Skidi, this plant is called *tukawia;* by another, the Chawi, it is called *tut.* It is said the seeds were cooked for food. This was the information given, but my informants may have mistaken this plant for the next one.

NELUMBO LUTEA (Willd.) Pers. Yellow Lotus, Water Chinquapin.
   (Pl. 10.)
   Tewape (Dakota).
   Tethawe (Omaha-Ponca).
   Tsherop (Winnebago).
   Tukawiu (Pawnee).

This is one of the plants considered to be invested with mystic powers. It is an important native food plant, both the seeds and the tubers being used. The plant was much sought and highly prized by the tribes living within its range. The hard, nutlike seeds were cracked and freed of their shells and used with meat for making soup. The tubers, also, after being peeled, were cut up and cooked with meat or with hominy. It contributes a delicious flavor, unlike any other.

The tubers were harvested by wading into the pond to search for them in the mud with the toes. When found, the mud was worked away from them with the feet, and they were pulled out by means of a hooked stick. In shape and general appearance they much resemble a small banana. This resemblance between the banana and *Nelumbo* tubers was remarked by the Omaha when bananas were first brought to their notice, so they were called *tethawe ega*ⁿ, " the things that look like *tethawe*," which is now the Omaha name of the banana. *Nelumbo* tubers might be cooked when first harvested, but to preserve them for winter use they were dried, being first peeled and cut into pieces about an inch long. An anatomical feature of the plant body is a ring of tubular air spaces extending longitudinally throughout the stem. This characteristic also pertains, naturally, to the tubers and gives rise to a droll notion in regard to them. The Indians say that one who is digging these tubers must be careful to refrain from snuffing through the nostrils, else the cavities of the tubers which he digs will become filled with mud and so spoiled. Another notion held in regard to this plant is that the tubers gathered by a tall man will be long, while a short man will get short tubers.

The Osages and other western natives employ the roots [sic] of this plant, . . . for food, preparing them by boiling. . . . Fully ripe, after a considerable boiling, they become as farinaceous, agreeable, and wholesome a diet as the potato. . . . This same species . . . is everywhere made use of by the natives, who collect both the nuts and roots. [1]

RANUNCULACEAE

THALICTRUM DASYCARPUM Fisch. & Lall.   Meadow Rue.   (Pl. 11, *a*.)

Wazimna (Dakota); *wazi*, " pine "; *mna*, " to smell."   The name seems to signify pinelike odor.

Nisude-hi (Omaha-Ponca), " flute-plant " (*nisude*, flute).

Skadiks or *skariks* (Pawnee).

By the Teton Dakota the fruits on approaching maturity in August are broken off and stored away for their pleasant odor; for this purpose they are rubbed and scattered over the clothing. The Indians say the effect is enhanced by dampness. This, like all other odors used by Indians, is of slight, evanescent fragrance. They used no heavy scents; all are delicate and give a suggestion of wholesomeness and of the freedom of the uncontaminated outdoors.

The hollow stems were used by small boys to make toy flutes (*nisude*). The Ponca sometimes used the tops as love charms. Bachelors rubbed the tops with saliva in the palms of the hands to give them power to capture the affections of the desired maidens by shaking hands with them. My informants said the plants of this species growing in Minnesota are better than those found in Nebraska.

The Pawnees used this plant as a stimulant for horses, causing them to snuff it into the nostrils when obliged to make forced marches of three or four days' duration in order to escape from enemies. For this purpose it was administered by rubbing it mixed with a certain white clay on the muzzle of the horse.

PULSATILLA PATENS (L.) Mill.   Pasque Flower, Twin-flower.   (Pl. 1, *a*.)

Hokshi-chekpa wahcha (Dakota), " Twin-flower."

As a counter-irritant for use in rheumatism and similar diseases the leaves of *Pulsatilla* were crushed and applied to cause a blister. This information was given by an old man of the Omaha tribe.

The people of the Dakota Nation call this plant by a name in their language which means " twin-flower," because usually each plant bears just two flowering scapes. Indians generally are keenly observant of all things in nature and reverent toward them. They have reverence and affection for the living creatures, the birds and beasts, the trees and shrubs and flowering plants. They have stories and songs about most of the plant and animal forms of life with

---

[1] Nuttall, Flora of Arkansas Territory, p. 160.

a. TUBERS AND FRUIT OF NELUMBO LUTEA

b. NELUMBO LUTEA, HABIT

Photo by courtesy of Department of Botany, Iowa State Agricultural College

a. THALICTRUM DIOICUM (EARLY MEADOW RUE). INDIAN USE OF THIS SPECIES THE SAME AS THAT OF T. PURPURASCENS

b. AQUILEGIA CANADENSIS

Photos by courtesy of George R. Fox, Appleton, Wis

which they are acquainted. They believe that each species has its own particular song which is the expression of its life or soul. The Song of the Twin-flower here given is translated from the Dakota language by Dr. A. McG. Beede.

> " I wish to encourage the children
> Of other flower nations now appearing
> All over the face of the earth;
> So while they awaken from sleeping
> And come up from the heart of the earth
> I am standing here old and gray-headed."

Pulsatilla is the very earliest bloomer in the spring, often appearing before the snow has disappeared. This fact explains the allusion in the words " I wish to encourage the children of other flower nations." The entire plant is hairy, and when ripe the head is white and bushy, having the appearance of a full and heavy growth of very white hair on the head of an old man. This appearance explains the allusion in " I am standing here gray-headed."

When an old Dakota first finds one of these flowers in the springtime it reminds him of his childhood, when he wandered over the prairie hills at play, as free from care and sorrow as the flowers and the birds. He sits down near the flower on the lap of Mother Earth, takes out his pipe and fills it with tobacco. Then he reverently holds the pipe toward the earth, then toward the sky, then toward the north, the east, the south, and the west. After this act of silent invocation he smokes. While he smokes he meditates upon all the changing scenes of his lifetime, his joys and sorrows, his hopes, his accomplishments, his disappointments, and the guidance which unseen powers have given him in bringing him thus far on the way, and he is encouraged to believe that he will be guided to the end. After finishing his pipe he rises and plucks the flower and carries it home to show his grandchildren, singing as he goes, The Song of the Twin-flower, which he learned as a child, and which he now in turn teaches to his grandchildren.

The mention of " reverently holding the pipe " is an allusion to a religious act of worship. Tobacco was used ceremonially and the pipe might be considered as a kind of censer. The earth was poetically and mystically regarded as Mother of all living things, all plants, animals, and human beings. The Sky likewise was regarded as Father, and the Cardinal Points as the Paths of approach of the Powers which are all about us in this world. Man is not apart from nor above nature but a part of nature. All good things in nature are his friends and kindred, and he should be friendly with all.

In the Omaha tribe, and probably also in other tribes, *Pulsatilla* had medicinal use. In cases of rheumatism and neuralgia the fresh leaves of *Pulsatilla* are crushed and applied on the surface over the affected part. It acts as a counter-irritant and will cause a blister if left on the skin long enough. My informant especially cautioned me that it must be used externally, as it would be dangerous and harmful if taken internally.

ANEMONE CANADENSIS L. Anemone, Wind Flower.

Te-zhinga-maka^n (Omaha-Ponca), "little buffalo medicine" (*te*, buffalo; *zhinga*, little; *maka^n*, medicine).

The root of this plant was one of the most highly esteemed medicines of the Omaha and Ponca. I do not know whether its value rested more on real physiological effects or on the great mystic powers ascribed to it; however, it was prescribed for a great many ills, especially wounds, by those who had the right to use it. It was applied externally and taken internally, and was used also as a wash for sores affecting the eyes or other parts. The right to use this plant belonged to the medicine-men of the *Te-sinde* gens. To touch a buffalo calf was taboo to this gens; hence the name of the plant, "little buffalo medicine." My informant, Amos Walker, of the *Te-sinde* gens of the Omaha, said that the plant is male and female, and that the flower of the male plant is white and that of the female red.

ANEMONE CYLINDRICA A. Gray. Long-fruited Anemone.

Wathibaba-maka^n (Ponca), "playing-card medicine."

Some Ponca used the woolly fruits of this plant as charms for good luck in playing cards, rubbing their hands in the smoke arising from burning some of the fruits and also rubbing the palms with the chewed fruit when about to engage in a card game.

AQUILEGIA CANADENSIS L. Wild Columbine. (Pl. 11, *b*.)

Inubtho^n-kithe-sabe-hi (Omaha-Ponca), "black perfume plant" (*inubtho^n*, fragrant; *kithe*, to make, to cause; *sabe*, black; *hi*, plant).

Skalikatit or *Skarikatit* (Pawnee), "black-seed" (*skali*, seed; *katit*, black).

The seeds are used by Omaha and Ponca, especially by bachelors, as a perfume. To obtain the odor the seeds must be crushed, a result which the Omaha commonly get by chewing to a paste. This paste is spread among the clothes, where its fragrant quality persists for a long time, being perceptible whenever dampened by dew or rain. Among the Pawnee the seeds are used for perfume and as a love charm. In cases of fever and headache the seeds are crushed with an elm-wood pestle in a mortar hollowed out of the same wood. The resulting powder is put into hot water and the infusion is drunk. For use as a love charm the pulverized seeds are rubbed in the palms, and the suitor contrives to shake hands with the desired one, whose fancy it is expected will thus be captivated. Omaha girls were somewhat in fear of the plant because of this supposed property and because, further, too strong a whiff of the odor was thought to cause nosebleed. On this account Omaha swains took delight in playfully frightening girls by suddenly thrusting some of the powder under their noses.

BERBERIDACEAE

CAULOPHYLLUM THALICTROIDES (L.) Michx. Blue Cohosh.
>   *Zhu-nakada-tanga-maka^n* (Omaha-Ponca), " great fever medicine " (*zhu*, flesh; *nakada*, hot; *tanga*, great; *maka^n*, medicine). *Zhu-nakada*, literally " hot flesh," is the Omaha word for " fever."

A decoction of the root was given for fevers. This was considered the most effectual febrifuge known to the Omaha.

MENISPERMACEAE

MENISPERMUM CANADENSE L. Moonseed.
>   *Ingthahe-hazi-i-ta* (Omaha-Ponca), " thunder grapes " (*ingthahe*, thunder; *hazi*, grapes; *i*, they; *ta*, genitive sign). Another name of *Menispermum* among the Ponca is *Wana^{n}ha hazi etai*, " grapes of the ghosts " (*wana^{n}ha*, ghost or shade or spirit; *hazi*, grapes).
>   *Wanaghi-haz* (Winnebago), literally " ghost fruit," or " fruit of the ghosts or shades."
>   *Hakakut* (Pawnee), " sore mouth " (*hakau*, mouth; *kut*, sore).

The several tribal names suggest the sinister character ascribed to this plant.

PAPAVERACEAE

SANGUINARIA CANADENSIS L. Bloodroot. (Pl. 12.)
>   *Minigathe maka^n wau* (Omaha-Ponca), " woman-seeking medicine."
>   *Peh-hishuji* (Winnebago). The first member of this compound means " gourd," and the second, " to make red "; hence the name probably refers to the use of the plant for reddening gourd rattles in ancient time, though I have never seen a rattle of modern time so decorated.

For the purpose of dyeing red the root of this plant was boiled with the materials to be dyed. For a love charm a bachelor of the Ponca after rubbing some of the root on his palm would contrive to shake hands with a girl he desired; if successful in this, after five or six days she would be found willing to marry him. From this use comes the Omaha-Ponca name of the plant. It was said to be used sometimes also as a decorative skin stain.

SAXIFRAGACEAE

GROSSULARIA MISSOURIENSIS (Nutt.) Cov. & Britt. Wild Gooseberry.
　　Wichaḱdeshka (Dakota) ; Yankton dialect, *wichaknaska;* Teton
　　dialect, *wichagnashka.*
　　Pezi (Omaha-Ponca).
　　Haz-ponoponoḱ (Winnebago), "crunching fruit" (*haz*, fruit;
　　ponoponoḱ, crunching).

The berries of this plant were used for food in their season. A
children's game was described among the Omaha in which the children were counted off into two parties. Each individual of both
parties was given a portion of the acidulous unripe berries which
he must try to eat without making a grimace. The party less successful in this ordeal had to pay a forfeit to the victorious party
or to execute some performance for their amusement, as for instance,
to hop on one foot so many steps backward.

RIBES AMERICANUM Mill. Wild Black Currant.
　　Chap-ta-haza (Dakota), " Beaver-berries," from *chapa-ta-haza*
　　(*chapa*, beaver; *haza*, berry; *ta*, genitive sign).
　　Pezi nuga (Omaha-Ponca) ; *pezi*, gooseberry; *nuga*, male.

An Omaha said a strong decoction of the root is made to drink as
a remedy for kidney trouble. A Winnebago medicine-man said the
root of the black currant is used by women for uterine trouble.

ROSACEAE

FRAGARIA VIRGINIANA Duchesne and F. AMERICANA (Porter) Britton.
　　Wild Strawberry. (Pl. 13, *a*.)
　　Wazhushtecha (Dakota). *Wazhushtecha-hu*, strawberry vine.
　　Wazhushtecha sha wi, the moon when strawberries are ripe,
　　June (*sha*, red; *wi*, moon, lunar month).
　　Bashte (Omaha-Ponca). *Bashte-hi*, strawberry vine.
　　Haz-shchek (Winnebago) ; *haz*, fruit.
　　Aparu-huradu (Pawnee), " ground berry " (*aparu*, berry; *huradu*,
　　ground).

All the tribes were fond of wild strawberries and luxuriated in
them in their season, but the fruit was too juicy to lend itself to
the process of drying successfully for winter use. Young leaves
of the plant were infused to make a beverage like tea by the Winnebago.

RUBUS OCCIDENTALIS L. and R. STRIGOSUS Michx. Wild Raspberry.
　　Takaⁿhecha (Dakota). *Takaⁿhecha-hu*, raspberry bush.
　　Agthamuⁿgi (Omaha-Ponca).
　　Aparu (Pawnee), berry.

a. SANGUINARIA CANADENSIS, DETAIL

Photo by courtesy of Public Museum of Milwaukee,
Department of Education

b. SANGUINARIA CANADENSIS, HABIT

Photo by courtesy of Department of Botany, Iowa State Agricultural College

a. WILD STRAWBERRY NATIVE TO WILD MEADOWS OF NEBRASKA

b. WOMAN OF THE TETON DAKOTA POUNDING CHOKECHERRIES (PADUS MELANO-
CARPA) TO DRY FOR WINTER SUPPLY

All the tribes used the berries for food, fresh in season, or dried for winter use. Young leaves were steeped to make a drink like tea.

According to an Omaha informant the root was used medicinally, for which purpose it was scraped and boiled; the decoction was given to children as a remedy for bowel trouble.

ROSA PRATINCOLA Greene. Wild Rose.

O^nzhi^nzhi^ntka (Dakota). *O^nzhi^nzhi^ntka-hu*, rosebush.

Wazhide (Omaha-Ponca).

Pahatu (Pawnee), red.

There are several species of *Rosa* in Nebraska, the most common being *Rosa pratincola*, the prairie rose. The fruits are sometimes eaten to tide over a period of food scarcity. An amusing instance is told in the Omaha tribe of a time when the people were without food and no game could be found. A man had been laboriously gathering for his family a supply of wild rose fruits. After he had a considerable quantity a man was seen returning with the carcass of a deer he had been able to kill. At once the rose fruits were cast away in prospect of the much more excellent food which had come to hand.

It is said that the inner bark of the rosebush was sometimes used for smoking, either alone or mixed with tobacco.

The Pawnee say there are sometimes large, brown hypertrophied growths on the lower part of the stems, which, when charred by fire and crushed to powder, were applied as a dressing to burns.

A wash for inflammation of the eyes was made by steeping the fruits, according to information from the Omaha.

THE SONG OF THE WILD ROSE

The following is a translation into English out of the Dakota language, by Dr. A. McG. Beede, of an old Dakota song. The people of the Dakota Nation, and other tribes also, think of the various plant and animal species as having each their own songs. With these people music—song—is an expression of the soul and not a mere artistic exercise.

Where the word " Mother " appears in the following song it refers to " Mother Earth," a living, conscious, holy being in Indian thought. The earth was truly venerated and loved by these people, who considered themselves not as owners or potential owners of any part of the land, but as being owned by the land which gave them birth and which supplied their physical needs from her bounty and satisfied their love of the beautiful by the beauty of her face in the landscape.

The trilled musical syllables at the close of the last two stanzas express the spontaneous joy which comes to a person who has " life-appreciation of Holy Earth."

The first stanza is an introduction by the narrator, not a part of the " Song of the Wild Rose." The remaining stanzas are the song of the Wild Rose itself:

> I will tell you of something I know,
> And you can't half imagine how good;
> It's the song of wild roses that grow
> In the land the Dakota-folk love.
>
> From the heart of the Mother we come,
> The kind Mother of Life and of All;
> And if ever you think she is dumb,
> You should know that flowers are her songs.
>
> And all creatures that live are her songs,
> And all creatures that die are her songs,
> And the winds blowing by are her songs,
> And she wants you to sing all her songs.
>
> Like the purple in Daydawn we come,
> And our hearts are so brimful of joy
> That whene'er we're not singing we hum
> Ti-li-li-li-i, ta-la-la-loo, ta-la-la-loo!
>
> When a maiden is ready to wed
> Pin wild roses all over her dress,
> And a rose in the hair of her head;
> Put new moccasins onto her feet.
> Then the heart of the Mother will give
> Her the songs of her own heart to sing;
> And she'll sing all the moons she may live,
> Ti-li-li-li-i, ta-la-la-loo, ta-la-la-loo!

MALUS IOENSIS (Wood) Britton. Crab Apple.
  She (Omaha-Ponca); *she-hi*, apple tree; *she-zho*^{n}, applewood; *she-si*, apple seed.

The crab apple was used for food by tribes having acquaintance with it. The Omaha and Ponca knew it as being found in the Oto country along the Missouri, in the southeast part of Nebraska. They said it is found nowhere west or north of this except on one creek which flows into the Niobrara River from the south at about the line between Knox and Holt Counties, 150 or 200 miles from any other locality where trees of this species grow. This would seem to indicate a case of plant migration by human agency, the occasion being the dropping in camp, in some place favorable for germination, of fruits or viable seeds brought with camp supplies obtained on a trip of considerable but not at all unusual distance to the southeast.

CRATAEGUS CHRYSOCARPA Ashe. Red Haw.

Taspaⁿ (Omaha-Ponca).

Chosaⁿwa (Winnebago).

The fruit was sometimes used for food, but commonly resorted to only as a famine food.

AMELANCHIER ALNIFOLIA Nutt. June Berry, Saskatoon.

Wipazuka (Dakota).

Zhoⁿ ḣuda (Omaha-Ponca), "gray wood" (*zhoⁿ*, wood; *ḣuda*, gray).

Haz-shutsh (Winnebago), "red-fruit" (*haz*, fruit; *shutsh*, red).

The berries were prized for food. The wood was used for arrow-shafts.[1]

PRUNUS AMERICANA Marsh. Wild Plum.

Kaⁿte (Dakota), plum; *kaⁿte-hu*, plum tree.

Kaⁿde (Omaha-Ponca), plum; *kaⁿde-hi*, plum tree.

Kantsh (Winnebago), plum; *kantsh-hu*, plum tree.

Niwaharit (Pawnee), plum; *Niwaharit-nahaapi*, plum tree.

The fruit was highly valued for food, being eaten fresh and raw or cooked as a sauce. The plums were also dried for winter use. They were commonly pitted before drying, but the Pawnee say they often dried them without removing the pits.

The Omaha planted their corn, beans, and squashes when the wild plum came into bloom.

A broom for sweeping the floor of the dwelling was made by binding together a bundle of plum twigs. The plum was used because of its toughness and elasticity.

An Omaha informant said the bark of the roots, after being scraped and boiled, was applied as a remedy for abrasions of the skin.

Sprouts or young growths of the wild plum are used by the Teton Dakota in making *wauⁿyaⁿpi*. This is an offering or form of prayer, consisting of a wand, made preferably from a wild-plum sprout peeled and painted. If painted, the design and color are emblematic. Near the top of the wand is fastened the offering proper, which may take the form of anything acceptable to the higher powers. A small quantity of smoking tobacco is an article very frequently used for this purpose. No matter how small a portion of the thing offered is used, the immaterial self of the substance is in it. Such offerings are usually made for the benefit of the sick. *Wauⁿyaⁿpi* may be made by anyone at any place if done with appropriate ceremony, but the most efficient procedure is to prepare an altar with due ceremony and there set the wand upright with the offering fastened near the top.[2]

---

[1] Riggs, Dakota-English Dictionary, p. 578.

[2] For this information I am indebted to Dr. J. R. Walker, Government physician at Pine Ridge, who has made very careful research into the ceremonies and rituals of the Teton Dakota.

PRUNUS BESSEYI Bailey. Sand Cherry. (Pl. 14.)

Aonyeyapi (Dakota). The Dakota have a saying that if a person gathering cherries moves in the direction contrary to the wind the cherries will be good and sweet, but on the other hand if he moves with the wind the cherries will be bitter and astringent. The name *aonyeyapi* expresses this idea.

Nonpa tanga (Omaha-Ponca), "big cherry."

Kus apaaru kaaruts (Pawnee), "cherry-sitting-hiding" (*kus*, cherry; *apaaru*, sitting; *kaaruts*, hiding).

Prunus besseyi is peculiarly indigenous to the Sand Hills area of Nebraska. The bush is small, varying in height as the situation is favorable or unfavorable to vegetation from less than 1 foot to 2½ feet. The fruits are purplish-black, 1.5 to 2 cm. in diameter, exceedingly prolific and varying in quality, some bushes bearing fruit somewhat astringent, others very desirable fruit.

All the tribes to whom the sand cherries were accessible made full use of them for food as a sauce during their fruiting season and laid up stores of them for winter by drying as they did the plums. An Oglala said these cherries produce fruit only about once in two years.

PADUS NANA (Du Roi) Roemer. Chokecherry. (Pl. 13, *b*.)

Chanpa (Dakota).

Nonpa-zhinga (Omaha-Ponca), "little cherry" (*nonpa*, cherry).

Nahaapi nakaaruts (Pawnee); *nakaaruts*, cherry; *nahaapi*, tree.

The fruit has long been highly esteemed by all the tribes for food; certain preparations of the cherry enter into old-time ceremonies and rituals as well as into stories, songs, and myths. In certain sleight-of-hand performances also this cherry is used. It is so highly esteemed as to give the name to one of the months in the Dakota calendar, *Canpa-sapa-wi*, "The-month-when-cherries-are-ripe" (literally, "black-cherry-moon").

The fruit was eaten with much relish while fresh and was dried for winter use. The gathering and drying of the fruit made a busy time for the community. The people traveled for miles to the streams along which the cherries were abundant. There they went into camp and worked at preparing the cherries while they lasted, or until as great a quantity as was required could be made ready. Since the pits were too small to be removed by any practicable method, the cherries were pounded to a pulp, pits and all, on stone mortars, and after being shaped into small cakes, were laid out to dry in the sun. A favorite food preparation of the Dakota is *wasna*, a sort of pemmican or mincemeat, the dried cherry forming the fruit for the compound.

b. BRANCH OF PRUNUS BESSEYI SHOWING PROLIFICNESS OF THIS FRUIT

a. FOLIAGE AND FRU T OF PRUNUS BESSEYI (SAND CHERRY)

The time of the Sun dance was determined by the ripening of the cherries. It began on the first day of the full moon when cherries were ripe.

A Ponca informant told me that a decoction of cherry bark was taken as a remedy for diarrhea. Another informant of the same tribe said a spoonful of the dried fruit very finely pulverized and infused in hot water was used as a remedy for the same ailment.

According to the latter informant, trappers washed their traps with water in which this bark had been boiled, in order to remove the scent of former captures.

PADUS MELANOCARPA (A. Nelson) Shafer. Western Chokecherry.

All that has just been said of *Padus nana* as to tribal nomenclature and uses applies equally to *Padus melanocarpa*.

MIMOSACEAE

ACUAN ILLINOENSIS (Michx.) Kuntze. Spider-bean.
Pezhe gasatho (Omaha-Ponca), " rattle plant " (*pezhe*, plant, herb; *gasatho*, rattle).
Atikatsatsiks (Pawnee), " spider-bean " (*atit*, bean; *tsatsiks*, spider; *ka*, inside). *Ati(t)ka tsatsiks*. Another name given is *kitsitsaris*, " bad plant " (*kits*, plant; *tsitsaris*, bad). *Kitsi(tsi)tsaris*.

When mature the entire plant with its persistent pods filled with seeds was used by little boys as a rattle when in play they mimicked some of the dances of their people.

The Pawnee boiled the leaves to make a wash to apply as a remedy for the itch.

CAESALPINIACEAE

GYMNOCLADUS DIOICA (L.) Koch. Kentucky Coffee-tree.
Waḣnaḣna (Dakota).
Naⁿtita (Omaha-Ponca).
Naⁿpashakanak (Winnebago).
Tohuts (Pawnee).

By the Dakota, Omaha, Ponca, Winnebago, and Oto the bark of the root after being dried was pulverized and, mixed with water, was used as a rectal injection in obstinate cases of constipation, for which it was said to be an infallible remedy. This remedy was used from time immemorial. Prior to contact with Europeans the Indians made their own syringes, an animal bladder being used for the bulb and a hollow cylindrical bone, as the leg bone of a prairie chicken, turkey, goose, or other bird, was used for the tube. The bulb was attached to the tube by sinew wrapping. When the pulverized bark was put into the water its action was carefully noted for a prognostication of the event. If the powder on touching the water started to circle to the right and gradually mixed, it was taken as a good omen for the recovery of the patient, but if the powder settled quietly to the bottom it was considered an omen of his death. A man whom I knew in the Omaha tribe had a very bad case of constipation, which was finally given up by the medicine-men of his own tribe, as they could not relieve him. A medicine-man of the Oto tribe, who was there on a visit, let it be known that he could cure the case, so he was called in and had complete success. One of the Omaha medicine-men, White Horse, wondered at the re-markable efficacy of the Oto remedy, purchased the secret, paying the Oto a horse and $20 in money for knowledge of this remedy, which he afterward imparted to me.

The pulverized bark of the root, if snuffed, causes uncontrollable sneezing. On account of this property it was used as a stimulant when a person was very sick and seemed near death, as in case of coma. If on application of the powder to the nostrils, the patient did not sneeze it was thought there was no hope of recovery. A Pawnee informed me that the dry pod of the plant, pulverized, was used to cause sneezing for the relief of headache.

The Pawnee roast the seeds and eat them as chestnuts are eaten. A Winnebago said the seeds after being pounded in a mortar were used for food.

A Santee Dakota said the root was sometimes used for making a black dye, but that it was not very good for the purpose. It was used as a dyestuff together with some component unknown to my informant. He said the root alone was without value.

The seeds are used by the Winnebago for counters or tally checks in gambling.

FABACEAE

BAPTISIA BRACTEATA Ell. Black Rattle-pod.

> *Tdika shande nuga* (Omaha-Ponca), male *tdika shande;* also called *gasatho*, rattle.
>
> *Pira-kari* (Pawnee); from *pirau*, children, and *kari*, many.

The first Omaha-Ponca name refers to the likeness of this plant to *Geoprumnon crassicarpum*, which is called *tdika shande. Baptisia,* being classed as similar to that but larger, more robust, is considered male. The second name refers to its use by small boys as a rattle when they play at having a dance. Pawnee boys used it in the same way. The Pawnee after pulverizing the seeds mixed the powder with buffalo fat as an ointment to be applied for colic by rubbing on the abdomen.

THERMOPSIS RHOMBIFOLIA (Nutt.) Richards. False Lupine.

The flowers of this plant were dried and used in fumigation, that is, the smoke treatment, for rheumatism, especially inflammatory rheumatism. The method of treatment was to mix the dried flowers with hair and burn the mixture under the affected part, confining the smoke and heat with a close covering. It is said that this treatment, with this remedy, reduces the swelling at once and relieves the pain.

MELILOTUS ALBA Desv. and M. OFFICINALIS (L.) Lam. Sweet Clover.

Wachaⁿga iyechecha (Dakota); wachaⁿga, sweet grass; iyechecha, similar.

Melilotus was introduced by the Europeans. Seeds probably came from the east among the effects of the early missionaries, for it first appeared on the grounds of the Presbyterian mission on the Omaha Reservation, which was built in 1856–57. The Omaha coming to the mission observed this plant, which had newly found its way into their country with the white men. They noticed that its odor resembled that of *Savastana odorata*, which they venerated and used in religious ceremonies. They were pleased with its odor, and since it was perhaps associated in their minds with the white man's religion, owing to its presence at the mission, they gathered bunches of it because of its pleasant odor, which they carried to their homes. Thus the plant was scattered all over the reservation, so that there is a more thorough distribution of it in that county than in any other part of the State that I have seen. The Dakota also are fond of the plant's odor and liken it to *Savastana*, hence their name for it. They gather bunches of *Melilotus* to hang in their houses for its fragrance.

ASTRAGALUS CAROLINIANA L. Little Rattle-pod.

Gaⁿsatho (Omaha-Ponca), rattle.

When ripe, the stalks with their persistent pods were used by small boys as rattles in the games in which they imitated the tribal dances, hence the Omaha-Ponca name signifying "rattle." No other use was found for the plant except to serve as a kind of mat on which was laid the fresh meat in course of butchering on the prairie, so that it might be kept free from dirt.

A decoction of the root was used among the Teton Dakota as a febrifuge for children.

GEOPRUMNON CRASSICARPUM (Nutt.) Rydb. Buffalo Pea, Ground Plum.

Pte ta wote (Dakota), "food of buffalo" (*pte*, buffalo; *wote*, food; *ta*, genitive sign).

Tdika shande (Omaha-Ponca) ; called also *wamide wenigthe* from a use that was made of it. *Wamide* means " seed " in the sense of seed designed for planting; *wenigthe* means " something to go with."

Both the Omaha and the Ponca in the old time gathered the fruits of this plant, which are formed just at corn-planting time, and put them with the seed corn. When the latter had been sufficiently soaked it was planted, but the *Geoprumnon* fruits were thrown away. No one in either tribe was able to give any reason for this process in preparation of seed corn; it was an old custom, the origin of which is forgotten.

Astragalus crassicarpus [1] was used as an ingredient of " war medicine " among the Chippewa. [2]

GLYCYRHIZA LEPIDOTA Pursh.   Wild Licorice.

Wi-nawizi (Dakota), " jealous woman " (*wi*, woman; *nawizi*, jealous). The name is said to have been suggested by the burs, which " take hold of a man."

Pithahatusakitstsuhast (Pawnee).

Among the Teton Dakota a poultice for sore backs of horses is made by chewing the leaves of this plant. For toothache the sufferer chews the root and holds it in the mouth. The Indians say, "It tastes strong at first, but after a while it becomes sweet." The leaves after being steeped are applied to the ears for earache. A decoction of the root is used as a remedy for fever in children.

PSORALEA ESCULENTA Pursh.   Pomme Blanche, Tipsin.   (Pls. 15, 16.)

Tipsin or *tipsinna* (Dakota) ; Teton dialect, *tipsinla*.

Nugthe (Omaha-Ponca).

Tdokewihi (Winnebago), hungry.

Patsuroka (Pawnee).

The roots of this plant were an important item of the vegetal diet of the Plains tribes. After being peeled they were eaten fresh and uncooked or cooked. Large quantities were dug in June and early July to peel and dry for the winter food supply. The peeled roots were braided in long strings by the tapering ends, as strings of garlic are braided by the tops.

The root is both farinaceous and glutinous and seems to form a desirable food with a palatable taste characteristic of the bean family.

Growing as this plant does, on the dry prairie in hard ground, with the enlargement of the root several inches below the surface, it

---

[1] *Astralagus crassicarpus* is a synonym of *Geoprumnon crassicarpum* (Nutt.) Rydb.

[2] Densmore, Chippewa Music—II, pp. 63–64.

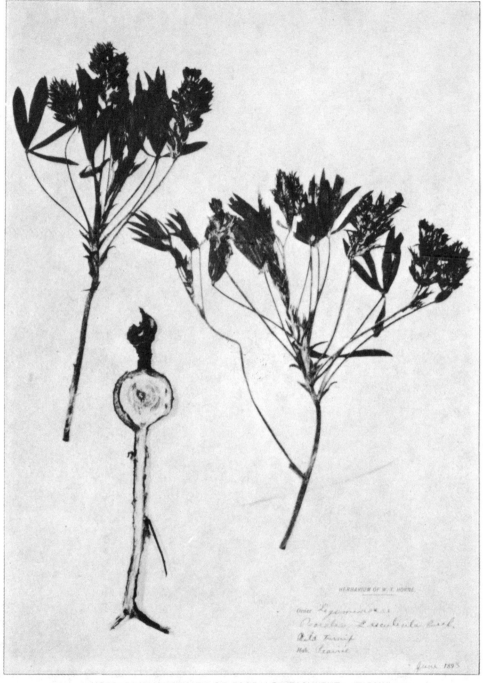

HERBARIUM SPECIMEN OF PSORALEA ESCULENTA (TIPSIN)

A STRING OF ROOTS OF PSORALEA ESCULENTA (TIPSIN) PEELED AND DRIED TO
PRESERVE FOR WINTER SUPPLY

is no easy task to harvest it. The top of the plant breaks off soon after ripening, and is blown away, scattering the seed, so the root is then almost impossible to find; hence it must be harvested before this occurs. The top usually has three or four branches. When the women and children go to the prairie to gather the roots, on finding a plant the mother tells the children to note the directions in which the several branches point and a child is sent in the general direction of each branch to look for another plant, for they say the plants "point to each other."

Psoralea has so important a place in the economy of the Plains tribes and has had for so long a time that it enters into their mythology, folklore, stories, and sleight-of-hand tricks. In the story "How the Big Turtle Went to War," as told in the Omaha tribe, it is said *Núg¢eúhuⁿ-biamá*, "*Psoralea* he cooked, they say." [1]

PSORALEA TENUIFLORA Pursh.

Tichanicha-hu (Dakota).

Among the Teton Dakota the root of this plant, with two others, the names of which I did not learn, were boiled together to make a medicine to be taken for consumption. Garlands were made of the tops, to be worn for protection of the head from the heat of the sun on very hot days.

AMORPHA FRUTICOSA L. False Indigo, Water-string.

Kitsuhast (Pawnee), "water-string" (*kitsu*, water; *hastu*, string).

Whenever possible to obtain it near the butchering place on the prairie this shrub was gathered and spread on the ground to receive the pieces of meat and keep them clean.

AMORPHA CANESCENS Pursh. Lead Plant, Shoestring.

Te-huⁿtoⁿ-hi (Omaha-Ponca), "buffalo bellow plant" (*te*, buffalo; *huⁿtoⁿ*, bellow; *hi*, plant). The name is derived from the fact that its time of blooming is synchronous with the rutting season of the buffalo, being at that season the dominant blooming plant on the prairie of the loess plain.

The stems were used by the Omaha for a moxa in cases of neuralgia and rheumatism. The small stems, broken in short pieces, were attached to the skin by moistening one end with the tongue. Then they were fired and allowed to burn down to the skin.

An Oglala said the leaves were sometimes used to make a hot drink like tea, and sometimes for smoking material. For this purpose after being dried and crushed fine they were mixed with a little buffalo fat.

---

[1] Dorsey ¢egiha Language, p. 256.

PAROSELA ENNEANDRA (Nutt.) Britton.

An Oglala informant said the root is poisonous. From her description of the effect I should think it must have a strong narcotic effect. I have not had an analysis made.

PAROSELA AUREA (Nutt.) Britton.

Pezhuta pa (Dakota), "bitter medicine."

An Oglala informant said a decoction of the leaves is used for colic and dysentery.

PETALOSTEMUM PURPUREUM (Vent.) Rydb. Purple Prairie Clover, and P. CANDIDUM (Willd.) Michx. White Prairie Clover.

Wanahcha (Dakota).

Maka^n skithe (Omaha-Ponca). This is one of several plants designated as *maka^n skithe*, sweet medicine.

Kiha piliwus hawastat (Pawnee), " broom weed " (*kiha*, room; *piliwus*, broom; *hawastatu*, weed). Also called *kahts-pidipatski*, small medicine (*kahts*, from *kahtsu*).

An Oglala said the leaves were sometimes used to make a drink like tea. According to a Ponca its root was commonly chewed for its pleasant taste. Although the word *maka^n* appears in the Omaha-Ponca name, no medicinal property is ascribed to this plant by these tribes so far as known now. The Pawnee name is derived from the use of the tough, elastic stems to make brooms with which to sweep the lodge. The plant was used in old time by the Pawnee as a prophylactic. The root, pulverized, was put into hot water. After the sediment settled the water was drunk to keep away disease. The sediment was collected in the drinking-shell and carried to a place prepared for it, where it was buried with respect.

GLYCINE APIOS L. Indian Potato. (Pl. 17.)

Mdo (Dakota) ; Teton dialect, *blo*.

Nu (Omaha-Ponca).

Tdo (Winnebago).

Its (Pawnee).

The tubers of this plant were utilized for food by all the tribes within its range. These tubers were prepared by boiling or roasting.

Apios tuberosa on the banks of streams and in alluvial bottoms is the true *pomme de terre* of the French and the modo or wild potato of the Sioux Indians, and is extensively used as an article of diet. . . . It should not be confounded with the ground-nut of the South.[1]

Many explorers and early settlers of Virginia, New England, and New France make mention of the use of *Apios*[2] as food by the

---

[1] Report of Commissioner of Agriculture for 1870, p. 405.
[2] *Glycine apios* was formerly called *Apios tuberosa*.

a. VINE OF GLYCINE APIOS (APIOS TUBEROSA)

Photo by courtesy of Public Museum of Milwaukee, Department of
Education

b. TUBERS OF GLYCINE APIOS (APIOS TUBEROSA)

a. SPECIMEN OF FALCATA COMOSA SHOWING LEAFY BRANCHES WITH PODS AND SMALL
BEANS PRODUCED THEREON FROM THE PETALIFEROUS FLOWERS.   *b.* LEAFLESS BRANCHES
WHICH GROW PROSTRATE ON GROUND SURFACE AND FOUR LARGE BEANS PRODUCED
UNDERGROUND FROM THE CLEISTOGAMOUS FLOWERS OF THESE LEAFLESS BRANCHES

various tribes in eastern North America, and not a few Europeans had recourse to it also for food.

Le Jeune says:

They eat, besides, roots, such as bulbs of the red lily; a root which has a taste of licorice; another that our French people call "Rosary," because it is distinguished by tubers in the form of beads; and some others.[1]

The Swedish botanist, Peter Kalm, in his journal, says:

Hopniss, or Hapniss, was the Indian name of a wild plant which they ate. . . . The Swedes in New Jersey and Pennsylvania still call it by that name, and it grows in the meadows in a good soil. The roots resemble potatoes, and were boiled by the Indians. . . . Mr. Bartram told me that the Indians who live farther in the country do not only eat these roots, which are equal in goodness to potatoes, but likewise take the peas which lie in the pods of this plant and prepare them like common peas.[2]

FALCATA COMOSA (L.) Kuntze. Ground Bean. (Pl. 18.)

Maka ta omnicha, or *o^nmnicha* (Dakota), "ground beans" (*maka,* ground; *o^nmnicha,* beans; *ta,* genitive sign).

Hi^nbthi-abe (Omaha-Ponca), "beans"; *hi^nbthi-hi,* bean-vines.

Honi^nk-boije (Winnebago).

Ati-kuraru (Pawnee), "ground beans" (*atit,* beans; *uraru,* earth, ground; *ku,* genitive sign).

Falcata grows in dense masses of vines over shrubbery and other vegetation in some places, especially along banks and the edge of timber. It forms two kinds of branches, bearing two forms of flower, producing two different fruits. Leafy branches climb over shrubbery, but under these, in the shade, prostrate on the earth, starting out from the base of the main stem, are leafless, colorless branches, forming a network on the surface of the ground. On these colorless, leafless branches cleistogamous flowers form, which push into the earth and there produce each a single bean closely invested by a membranaceous pod. Each of these beans is from 10 mm. to 17 mm. in long diameter, inclined to be flat, and from 5 mm. to 10 mm. thick. The pods produced from the petaliferous flowers on the upper leafy branches of the vine are 15 mm. to 20 mm. long and contain four or five dark, mottled, diminutive beans about the size of lentils. No attention is paid to these small aerial beans, but the large subterranean beans were eagerly sought as an article of food on account of their agreeable taste and nutritive value. From these qualities they contributed a considerable item in the dietary of the tribes.

Voles dig them and garner them into hoards of a pint or more in a place, and the women would appropriate part of the voles' stores

---

[1] Le Jeune's "Relation," in *Jesuit Relations,* vol. VI, p. 273..
[2] Peter Kalm, Travels into North America, vol. I, pp. 385–386.

to their own use. The Pawnee formerly inhabited the larger part of Nebraska with villages on the Loup, the Platte, and the Republican Rivers. In 1875 they were removed to Oklahoma, where they now reside. Mr. James R. Murie, of that tribe, in a letter of February 15, 1913, referring to *Falcata*, a specimen of which had been sent him, said:

We call them *atikuraru* . . . The Pawnees ate them. In winter time the women robbed rats' [sic] nests and got big piles of them. Nowadays when the old women see lima beans they say they look like *atikuraru* in Nebraska.

Women of the Dakota Nation say that they not only obtained the large ground beans of this species, garnered by the voles, or " wood mice," but that they also gathered the small beans produced in large quantity on the upper branches of the same vine from petaliferous blossoms. These smaller beans are about the size of lentils. The large beans, produced from cleistogamous blossoms on leafless branches spreading prostrate on the ground under the cover of the upper branches, are about the size of lima beans, and grow at a depth of an inch or two under the ground in the manner of peanuts.

A most interesting item in connection with this food plant is the statement of the women of the Dakota Nation that they did not take the ground beans from the stores of the little animals which gathered them without giving some food commodity in return. They said it was their custom to carry a bag of corn with them when they went to look for the stores of beans gathered by the animals, and when they took out any beans they put in place of them an equal quantity of corn. They say that sometimes instead of corn they put some other form of food acceptable to the animals in place of the beans which they took away. They said it would be wicked to steal from the animals, but they thought that a fair exchange was not robbery.

Father De Smet, the indefatigable Christian missionary to the tribes of the upper Missouri, makes the following observation:

The earth pea and bean are also delicious and nourishing roots [sic], found commonly in low and alluvial lands. The above-named roots form a considerable portion of the sustenance of these Indians during winter. They seek them in the places where the mice and other little animals, in particular the ground-squirrel, have piled them in heaps. [1]

PHASEOLUS VULGARIS L. Garden Bean.

O^{n}mnicha (Dakota).

Hi^{n}bthi^{n}ge (Omaha-Ponca).

Honi^{n}k (Winnebago).

Atit (Pawnee).

The garden bean in all its many types and varieties is one of the gifts of the Western Hemisphere to the world. The earliest ex-

[1] De Smet, Life and Travels, vol. II, p. 655.

plorers tell of finding them in cultivation among the tribes of North America from Quebec southward through Mexico and Central America into most of South America. Dr. D. V. Havard says:

The common kidney bean (*Phaseolus vulgaris* Savi) is a South American plant . . . The finding of seeds of this species by Prof. Witmack in the prehistoric graves of Arizona, not only completed the demonstration of its American origin but likewise proved the antiquity of its culture in our own country.[1]

In considering the cultivated plants grown by the tribes of Nebraska at the time of the advent of Europeans it is of interest to discover the probable region or regions of their origin and first domestication. We find the most advanced civilization on the continent prior to European invasion was in Mexico and southward. In that direction also we find the wild plants most nearly related to the species aboriginally cultivated both there and in what is now the United States, facts suggesting the probable area inhabited by their wild prototypes. Doctor Coulter[2] reports nine species of the genus *Phaseolus* indigenous to western Texas, some or all of which, judging from their size as he describes them, seem to make promising candidates for domestication, and we can conjecture that some of these or others farther south were the original of the cultivated varieties found here.

Before the coming of white men the Omaha cultivated many varieties of beans of different sizes and colors, both bush beans and climbing beans. The pole beans they called *hiⁿbthiⁿge amoⁿthiⁿ* (*hiⁿbthiⁿge*, bean; *amoⁿthiⁿ*, walking). Bush beans were called *hiⁿbthiⁿge moⁿthiⁿ azhi*, "bean not walking" (*azhi*, not). Since their old order of life and industries have been broken up by the incursion of Europeans they have lost the seed of a number of varieties which they formerly grew, but I have found four varieties still grown by them, and they can remember and describe the following fifteen: 1. Black-spotted; 2. White-spotted; 3. Yellow-spotted; 4. Red-spotted; 5. Gray-spotted; 6. Very red; 7. Very black; 8. A sort of dark-red; 9. White; 10. A sort of dark-blue; 11. A sort of dark-yellow; 12. White with red around the hilum; 13. White with black around the hilum; 14. Blue, somewhat spotted; 15. "Like the hair of an elk," somewhat yellow-gray.

LESPEDEZA CAPITATA Michx. Rabbit-foot.

Te-huⁿtoⁿ-hi nuga (Omaha-Ponca), "male buffalo bellow plant" (*te*, buffalo; *huⁿtoⁿ*, bellow; *nuga*, male). *Amorpha canescens* was considered *te-huⁿtoⁿ-hi miga*, female *te-huⁿtoⁿ-hi*.

Parus-as (Pawnee); *parus*, rabbit; *as*, foot.

The Pawnee name will be recognized as an appropriate descriptive name. The Omaha and Ponca used the stems as they did those of

---

[1] Havard, Food Plants of North American Indians, p. 99.
[2] Coulter, Botany of Western Texas, pp. 89–90.

Amorpha canescens for moxa. *Amorpha* they found in the sandy loam soil of valleys and *Lespedeza* on the hills of the loess plain.

LATHYRUS ORNATUS Nutt. Wild Sweet Pea.

Hi^{n}bthi-si-tanga (Omaha-Ponca), large-seeded *hi^{n}bthi* bean (*si*, seed; *tanga*, large).

My informants could describe it and tell in what locality it is to be found. They remembered it as they formerly saw it in the Sand Hills when they went there on the hunt. Children sometimes gathered the pods, which they roasted and ate in sport. The plant was not considered of any importance, although noted and named.

OXALIDACEAE

IONOXALIS VIOLACEA (L.) Small. Sheep Sorrel, Violet Wood Sorrel, and XANTHOXALIS STRICTA (L.) Small. Yellow Wood Sorrel.

Hade-sathe (Omaha-Ponca), " sour herb " (*hade*, herb, grass; *sathe*, sour).

Pawnee: Various names were given. *Skidadihorit*, a name having reference to its taste, which they describe as "sour like salt"; some called it *kait*, salt; another name given was *askirawiyu; as*, foot; *kira*, water; *wiyu*, stands. Another name given is *kisosit*. The Pawnee say that the buffalo was very fond of *Xanthoxalis stricta*. Children ate both species, especially *Ionoxalis violacea*, leaves, flowers, scapes, and bulbs. The bulbs were pounded and fed to horses to make them fleet.

LINACEAE

LINUM LEWISII Pursh. Wild Flax.

The seeds of the wild blue flax were gathered and used in cookery both because of their highly nutritive value and for the agreeable flavor which they added to that with which they were cooked.

RUTACEAE

ZANTHOXYLUM AMERICANUM Mill. Prickly Ash.

Hakusits (Pawnee), thorn.

Omaha young men used the fruits of this shrub as a perfume. By the Pawnee the fruits were used as a remedy for horses in case of retention of urine.

MELIACEAE

MELIA AZEDERACH L. China Berry.

Maka^{n}zhide sabe (Omaha-Ponca), "black ' red-medicine.' "

Introduced into the Southern States early in the nineteenth century, it has become naturalized, growing freely along the streams of

Oklahoma. It has large, smooth black seeds inclosed in the waxy, yellow translucent fruits, which are borne in great profusion. The seeds have been utilized for beads by the tribes acquainted with them. The Omaha traveling into Oklahoma have found them there, and have taken up their use. They already had employed for beads as well as for a good-luck charm the bright red seed of a species of *Erythrina*. They say it grows somewhere to the southwest, toward or in Mexico. They call it "red medicine," *maka*[n] *zhide* (*maka*[n], medicine; *zhide*, red). When the seeds of *Melia* were adopted for use as beads they likened them to *maka*[n] *zhide*, and so call them *maka*[n]-*zhide sabe*, "black red-medicine."

EUPHORBIACEAE

CROTON TEXENSIS (Klotzsch) Muell. Arg.

One Pawnee informant said that very young babies, when sick, were bathed with a decoction of leaves of this plant.

CHAMAESYCE SERPYLLIFOLIA (Pers.) Small.

Naze-ni pezhi (Omaha-Ponca), "milkweed" (*naze-ni*, milk; *pezhi*, weed or herb).

According to a Ponca informant this plant was boiled and the decoction drunk by young mothers whose flow of milk was scanty or lacking, in order to remedy that condition. This use of the plant is probably prescribed according to the doctrine of signatures. An Omaha informant said it was used as a remedy in case of dysentery and abdominal bloating in children. For this purpose the leaves of the plant were dried and pulverized and applied after first crosshatching the abdomen with a knife and then further abrading the skin with the head of a certain plant, the identity of which I do not know at present as I have not had a sample. Then the pulverized leaves were rubbed by hand on the abraded surface. It was said to cause a painful, smarting sensation and to act powerfully upon the bowels through the intervening tissues and to give relief.

An Oglala informant said little boys used the plant in play as a headdress.

DICHROPHYLLUM MARGINATUM (Pursh) Kl. & Garcke. Snow-on-the-mountain.

Karipika or *kalipika tsitsiks* (Pawnee); *tsitsiks*, "poison."

Karipika or *kalipika* is the Pawnee name of *Asclepias syriaca*, to which they compare this plant, because of its milky juice, but they recognize the poisonous quality of all the genus.

ANACARDIACEAE

RHUS GLABRA L. Smooth Sumac. (Pl. 19, *a*.)

Cha[n]-*zi* (Dakota), "yellow-wood" (*zi*, yellow).

Mi[n]*bdi-hi* (Omaha-Ponca).

Haz-ni-hu (Winnebago), "water-fruit bush" (*haz*, fruit; *ni*, water; *hu*, plant, tree, bush).

Nuppikt (Pawnee), "sour top."

In the fall when the leaves turned red they were gathered and dried for smoking by all the tribes. Omaha and Winnebago both said the roots were used to make a yellow dye. Among the Pawnee the fruits were boiled to make a remedy for dysmenorrhea and also for bloody flux. An Omaha medicine-man, White Horse, said the fruits were boiled to make a styptic wash to stop hemorrhage in women after parturition, and that a decoction of the root was used to drink in case of retention of urine and when urination was painful. An Omaha said that a poultice made by bruising the leaves was applied wet in case of poisoning of the skin, as by some irritant vegetal oil. In case the leaves could not be had the fruits were soaked and bruised, the application being kept moist with the water in which the fruits had been soaked.

TOXICODENDRON TOXICODENDRON (L.) Britton. Poison Oak, Poison Ivy.

Ḣthi-wathe-hi (Omaha-Ponca), "plant that makes sore" (*ḣthi*, sore; *wathe*, to make; *hi*, plant, bush, tree, any plant body).

The people knew and dreaded the poisonous effects of this plant, but I did not learn of any use for it, nor of any antidote for its poison.

ACERACEAE

ACER SACCHARUM Marsh. Hard Maple.

Chaⁿ-ha saⁿ (Dakota), "pale-bark" (*chaⁿ-ha*, bark; *saⁿ*, pale or whitish).

Naⁿ-saⁿk (Winnebago), "pure or genuine wood" (*naⁿ*, wood; *saⁿk*, real, genuine).

This species was used in Minnesota by the Santee Dakota. Since their removal to Nebraska in 1866 they have made use of the next species.

ACER SACCHARINUM L. Soft Maple.

Tahado (Dakota).

Wenu-shabethe-hi (Omaha-Ponca), "tree to dye black."

Wissep-hu (Winnebago), "tree to dye black."

All the tribes made sugar from the soft maple. The Dakota word for sugar is *chaⁿhaⁿpi*, literally "wood" or "tree juice" (*haⁿpi*, juice). The Omaha word is *zhoⁿni* (*zhoⁿ*, wood or tree; *ni*, water). The Pawnee word for sugar, *nakits*, is also compounded of their words for "tree" (*nakis*) and "water" (*kiitsu*). From these examples it appears that the etymology of the word for "sugar" in the

a. CLUSTERS OF FRUITS OF RHUS GLABRA

Photo by courtesy of Department of Botany, Iowa State Agricultural
College

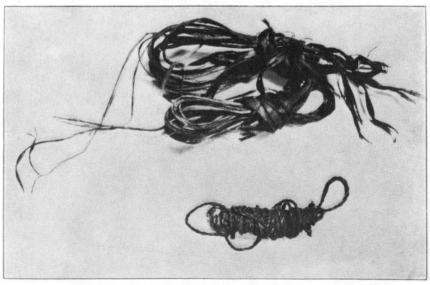

b. CORDAGE MADE FROM INNER BARK OF TILIA AMERICANA (BASSWOOD); A
BUNDLE OF RAW FIBER AND A PIECE OF CORD MADE BY HAND FROM THE FIBER

languages of the several tribes is evidence of the aboriginal source of the article, for if they had first gotten sugar from the traders' stores it would not have been associated in their minds with the sap of trees.

Prince Maximilian of Wied, in his journey up the Missouri River in the spring of 1832, observed the process of sugar making. In his journal of the latter part of April of that year he says, "Auch die freien Indianer benutzten jenen Ahorn zur Bereitung des Zuckers."[1]

The Omaha and Winnebago names of this tree are given from the use of maple twigs to make a black dye. The twigs and bark of new growth were boiled. A certain clay containing an iron compound, found interstratified with the Pierre shales exposed along the Niobrara River, was mixed with grease and roasted. This roasted clay and the water in which the bark was boiled were then mixed, and the tanned hides which were to be dyed were soaked for two or three days to get the right color. Treatment for a short time made them brown, and for a longer time black.

ACER NEGUNDO L. Boxelder.

Tashkada^n (Dakota). In the Teton dialect it is called by either the name *tashkada^n* or *cha^n-shushka*.

Zhaba-ta-zho^n (Omaha-Ponca), beaver-wood (*zhaba*, beaver: *zho^n*, wood; *ta*, genitive sign).

Nahosh (Winnebago).

Ósako (Pawnee).

This tree was used also for sugar making by all the tribes. The Dakota and Omaha and probably the other tribes used boxelder wood to make charcoal for ceremonial painting of the person and for tattooing.

Previous information as to the making of sugar from the sap of this tree pertained, among the Pawnee and Omaha, only to times now many years in the past; but it has been found that among some tribes sugar is still made from this source. In September, 1916, the writer found a grove of trees on the Standing Rock Reservation in North Dakota, of which every tree of any considerable size showed scars of tapping which had been done the previous spring in sugar making.

BALSAMINACEAE

IMPATIENS PALLIDA Nutt. and I. BIFLORA Walt. Wild Touch-me-not.

The stems and leaves of this plant were crushed together to a pulp and applied to the skin as a remedy for rash and eczema by the Omaha.

---

[1] Maximilian, Reise in das Innere Nord-America, vol. 1, p. 279. "All the free Indians employ that maple for sugar-making."

RHAMNACEAE

CEANOTHUS AMERICANUS L.   Red Root, Indian Tea.
  Tabe-hi (Omaha-Ponca).
The leaves were used by all the tribes to make a drink like tea.
The taste is something like that of the Asiatic tea and is much better
than that of the South American yerba maté.   On the buffalo hunt,
when timber was scarce, the great gnarled woody roots of this shrub,
often much larger than the part above ground, were used for fuel.

VITACEAE.

VITIS CINEREA Engelm. and V. VULPINA L.   Wild Grape.
  *Hasta*n*ha*n*ka* (Dakota); Teton dialect *Cha*n *wíyape*.   The Teton
    name simply means vine (*cha*n, tree; *wíyape*, twine, tree-twiner).
  Hazi (Omaha-Ponca).   Grape vine, *hazi-hi*.
  Hapsintsh (Winnebago).
  Kisúts (Pawnee).
The fruit was used for food, either fresh or dried for winter use.
A Pawnee said he had seen people tap large grapevines in spring
and collect the sap to drink fresh.   He said it tasted like grape juice.

PARTHENOCISSUS QUINQUEFOLIA (L.) Planch.   Virginia Creeper,
    False Grape.
  *I*n*gtha hazi itai* (Omaha-Ponca), ghost grapes (*hazi*, grapes).

CELASTRACEAE

EUONYMUS ATROPURPUREA Jacq.   Burning Brush.
  *Wana*n*ḣa-i-mo*n*thi*n (Omaha-Ponca), " ghost walking-stick."
A Winnebago medicine-man said women drink a decoction of the
inner bark for uterine trouble.

CELASTRUS SCANDENS L.   Bitter-sweet.
  Zuzecha-ta-wote (Dakota), " snake-food " (*zuzecha*, snake; *wote*,
    food; *ta*, genitive sign).
An Oglala called it snake-food and held the notion that it is
poisonous.

TILIACEAE

TILIA AMERICANA L.   (Pl. 19, *b*.)
  *Hi*n*ta-cha*n (Dakota).
  Hinde-hi (Omaha-Ponca).
  *Hi*n*shke* (Winnebago).
The inner bark fiber was used by the Omaha and Ponca for making
cordage and ropes.   The Pawnee say it was employed also for spin-
ning cordage and weaving matting.

MALVACEAE

CALLIRRHOE INVOLUCRATA (T. & G.) A. Gray. Purple Mallow.

Short Bull, a half Brulé, half Oglala, called this plant *Pezhuta nⁿtiazilia*, " smoke treatment medicine " (*pezhuta*, medicine; *nⁿtiazilia* having reference to its use to produce smoke for medical use). Fast Horse, an Oglala, called it *pezhuta*, " medicine."

Among the Teton Dakota this plant was used for the smoke treatment. The dried root having been comminuted and fired, the smoke was inhaled for cold in the head, and aching parts were bathed in it. The root was boiled, the decoction being drunk for internal pains.

MALVASTRUM COCCINEUM (Pursh) A. Gray. Red False Mallow.

Heyoka ta pezhuta (Dakota), " medicine of the *heyoka* " (*pezhuta*, medicine; *heyoka*, a dramatic order among the Dakota; *ta*, the genitive sign).

This plant possesses to a large degree the mucilaginous property which is in some degree common to all species of this family. On account of this property the Dakota *heyoka* utilized it by chewing it to a paste, which was rubbed over hands and arms, thus making them immune to the effect of scalding water, so that to the mystification and wonderment of beholders these men were able to take up pieces of hot meat out of the kettle over the fire.

The plant was also chewed and applied to inflamed sores and wounds as a cooling and healing salve.

VIOLACEAE

VIOLA SP.

Among the Omaha children violets were used in playing a game. In springtime a group of children would gather a quantity of violets; then, dividing into two equal parties, one party took the name of their own nation and the other party took another, as for instance Dakota. The two parties sat down facing each other, and each player snapped violets with his opponent till one or the other had none remaining. The party having the greater number of violets remaining, each party having had an equal number at the beginning, was the victor and playfully taunted the other as being poor fighters.

LOASACEAE

NUTTALLIA NUDA (Pursh) Greene.

Toka hupepe (Dakota).

The stems, after being stripped of their leaves, were pounded to extract the gummy yellow juice. This was applied externally as a remedy for fever after it had been boiled and strained.

CACTACEAE

OPUNTIA HUMIFUSA Raf.   Prickly Pear.   (Pl. 20, *a*.)
U^nchela (Dakota).   The fruits are called *u^nchela taspu^n*.
Pidahatus (Pawnee).

An amusing summer game played by small boys of the Dakota
Nation was the "cactus game." Boys gathered on the prairie where
the cactus abounded. One boy who was a swift runner was chosen
"to be it," as white children say in games. This boy would take
a cactus plant and impale it on a stick. The stick served as a handle
by which he held up the plant for the other boys to shoot with their
bows and arrows. When a boy hit the target the target holder ran
after him and would strike him with the spiny cactus; then he would
return to the goal and receive the shots of other boys. Thus the
game continued indefinitely at the pleasure of the players.

The fruits were eaten fresh and raw after the bristles had been
removed, or they were stewed. They were also dried for winter use.
Sometimes from scarcity of food the Indians had to resort to the
stems, which they roasted after first removing the spines. The
mucilaginous juice of the stems was utilized as a sizing to fix the
colors painted on hides or on receptacles made from hides. It was
applied by rubbing a freshly peeled stem over the painted object.
On account of this mucilaginous property the peeled stems were
bound on wounds as a dressing.

LOPHOPHORA WILLIAMSII (Lem.) Coulter.   Peyote.
Maka^n (Omaha-Ponca).   The medicine.

The religious cult associated with this plant has been introduced
among the Nebraska tribes from others to the southward. The plant
is indigenous to the Rio Grande region, where its cult arose. Thence
it spread from tribe to tribe, even to our northern national boundary.
This plant is often popularly but erroneously called mescal. The
use of peyote and the religious observances connected with it were
introduced among the Omaha in the winter of 1906–07 by one of
the tribe who returned from a visit to the Oto in Oklahoma. He
had been much addicted to the use of alcohol and had heard among
the Oto that this religion would cure him. The cult had already
been introduced into the Winnebago tribe, whose reservation adjoins
that of the Omaha, so when he reached home he sought the advice
and help of the leader of the Peyote Society in that tribe. A society
was soon formed in the Omaha tribe, and although at first much
opposed it grew till it absorbed half the tribe. At the present time
its influence has somewhat weakened.

The peyote plant and its cult appeal strongly to the Indian's sense
of the mysterious and occult. The religious exercises connected with

a. A CACTUS NATIVE TO NEBRASKA

b. GATHERING BUFFALO BERRIES (LEPARGYRAEA ARGENTEA)

it are attended by much circumstance of ceremony and symbolism. The average Indian, with his psychic inheritance and his physical and psychic environment, naturally attributes to the peyote most wonderful mystic powers. As the Semitic mind could conceive, and the Aryan mind could accept the Semitic conception, that deity may be incarnated in an animal body—that is, a human body—so to the American Indian mind it seems just as reasonable to conceive that deity may dwell in a plant body. So he pays the plant divine honors, making prayers to it or in connection with it, and eating it or drinking a decoction of it in order to appropriate the divine spirit—to induce the good, and exorcise the evil. In brief, the use of peyote by the Indian corresponds to the Christian use of bread and wine in the eucharist.

The body of doctrine and belief connected with this cult is a curious blending of aboriginal American religious ideas with many imbibed by the Indians from Christian missionaries. In the meeting places the worshipers gather in a circle about a fireplace in the center of the lodge or tent. A fire is kept up throughout the meeting. At the west side of the fire sits the leader. In front of him is spread a cloth like an altar cloth; on this lies a peyote top, and at the edge nearest to the leader an open Bible. At his right hand stands a staff symbolically decorated with feather ornamentation. In his hand he carries a fan made of 12 eagle feathers symbolizing the 12 Christian apostles. A water drum is beaten with a low insistent thrumming sound, accompanied by a gourd rattle, while songs are chanted, and the people gaze into the fire or sit with bowed head. Owing to the hypnotic effect of the firelight, the community of thought, abstraction from all extraneous affairs, the droning chant, the thrumming of the drum, and the mental attitude of expectancy induced by the words of the speakers, who discourse on the visions which shall be seen, combined with the physiological effect of the drug, which stimulates the optic center, the people fancy they really see most wonderful visions of spirits. As an example, the vision described by a certain Omaha may be related. It will be observed that his vision was the result of the juxtaposition of a number of experiences and mental processes recalled and immediately induced by the circumstances of the meeting and the physiologic action of the drug. He was an ordinary reservation Indian, who had had some schooling and had been in Washington and other eastern cities. On this occasion the opening reading from the Bible had been the story of the Hebrew prophet taken up to heaven in a chariot of fire. The Indian fell into a trancelike state and afterwards described his vision. He related that Jesus had come for him in an automobile and had taken him up to heaven, where he had seen God in His glory in a splendid city, and with God he had seen many of the great men of all time, more than he could remember.

ELAEAGNACEAE

LEPARGYREA ARGENTEA (Nutt.) Greene. Buffalo-berry. (Pl. 20, *b*.)
  Mashti^{n}cha-puté (Dakoṭa), "rabbit-nose" (*mashti^{n}cha*, rabbit; *puté*, nose).
  Zho^n-hoje-wazhide (Omaha-Ponca), or *wazhide ḳuta*, gray *wazhide*,
  Haz-shutz (Winnebago), "red-fruit" (*haz*, fruit; *shutz*, red).
  Laritsits (Pawnee).

The fruits are used fresh in season and are dried for winter use. The fruit was ceremonially used in feasts given in honor of a girl arriving at puberty. *Padus nana* was ordinarily used, but *Lepargyrea* might be substituted. This was a custom among the Dakota.[1]

ARALIACEAE

PANAX QUINQUEFOLIUM L. Ginseng.

A Pawnee gave the information that ginseng roots in composition with certain other substances were used as a love charm. From various individuals the information was gathered bit by bit severally and adduced, showing that the four species of plants used in compounding this love charm were *Aquilegia canadensis*, *Lobelia cardinalis*, *Cogswellia daucifolia*, and *Panax quinquefolium* or possibly a species of *Ligusticum*. Specimens of the latter were not in hand, but informants spoke of it as *Angelica*. They had become acquainted with *Angelica* of the pharmacists and probably mistook it for their own native *Ligusticum*. It is possible that various combinations of four plants might have been used, but it appears certain that *Aquilegia canadensis* and *Cogswellia daucifolia* were considered most potent. The parts used were seeds of *Aquilegia* and *Cogswellia*, dried roots of *Panax*, and dried roots and flowers of *Lobelia cardinalis*. With these vegetal products was mingled red-earth paint. The possession of these medicines was supposed to invest the possessor with a property of attractiveness to all persons, in spite of any natural antipathy which might otherwise exist. When to these were added hairs obtained by stealth through the friendly offices of an amiably disposed third person from the head of the woman who was desired, she was unable to resist the attraction and soon yielded to the one who possessed the charm.

---

[1] Dorsey, Siouan Cults, p. 483.

APIACEAE

WASHINGTONIA LONGISTYLIS (Torr.) Britton. Sweet Cicely.

Chaⁿ-pezhuta (Dakota); *chaⁿ*, wood; *pezhuta*, medicine.

Shaⁿga-makaⁿ (Omaha-Ponca), horse-medicine.

Kahtstaraha (Pawnee), "buffalo medicine" (*kahtsu*, medicine; *taraha*, buffalo).

The Omaha and Ponca say that horses were so fond of the roots of *Washingtonia* that if one whistled to them, while holding out the bag of roots, the horses came trotting up to get a taste, and so could easily be caught. An Omaha said that the roots were pounded up to make poultices to apply to boils. A Winnebago medicine-man reported the same treatment for wounds. A Pawnee said that a decoction of the roots was taken for weakness and general debility.

HERACLEUM LANATUM Michx. Cow Parsnip, Beaver Root. (Pl. 21.)

Zhaba-makaⁿ (Omaha-Ponca), "beaver medicine" (*zhaba*, beaver; *makaⁿ*, medicine).

A Winnebago medicine-man said the tops of this plant were used in the smoke treatment for fainting and convulsions. According to a Pawnee, the root, scraped or pounded fine and boiled, was applied as a poultice for boils. It was learned from an old Omaha woman that the root was boiled and the decoction taken for intestinal pains and as a physic. An old Omaha medicine-man said the dried roots were pounded fine and mixed with beaver dung, and that the mixture was placed in the hole in which the sacred pole was planted.

COGSWELLIA DAUCIFOLIA (Nutt.) M. E. Jones. Love Seed.

Pezhe bthaska (Omaha-Ponca), "flat herb" (*pezhe*, herb; *bthaska*, flat).

Seeds of this aromatic plant with seeds and various parts of other plants were used as a love charm by men of all tribes in the Plains region. A Pawnee stated that to carry seeds of *Cogswellia* rendered the possessor attractive to all persons, so he would have many friends, all people would serve him well, and if used in connection with certain other plants would make him winning to women, so he might win any woman he might desire.

CORNACEAE

CORNUS AMOMUM Mill. Red Dogwood, Kinnikinnick. (Pl. 22.)

Chaⁿ-shasha (Dakota), "red wood" (*chaⁿ*, wood; *shasha*, a reduplication of *sha*, red). So called from the winter coloration of its bark.

Ninigahi (Omaha-Ponca). Contracted from *nini*, pipe, and *igahi*, to mix; to mix [with tobacco] for the pipe.

Ruĥi-shutsh (Winnebago).

Rapahat (Pawnee), "red-stick" (*ra*, stick; *pahat*, red).

The outer bark was removed, after which the inner bark was scraped and dried for smoking. It is fragrant, and all the tribes were very fond of it.

CORNUS STOLONIFERA Michx. Red Brush, Kinnikinnick.

Cha^n-shasha-hi^{n}chake (Dakota), real *cha^n-shasha* (*hi^{n}chake*, real, very, indeed).

Ninigahi ĥte (Omaha-Ponca), real *ninigahi*.

This species is preferred for smoking. It is said to be the best of all, but the Indians describe and name another which was also used, but which I did not succeed in seeing or identifying. The Omaha and Ponca call it *ninigahi gthezhe*, "spotted *ninigahi*."

CORNUS ASPERIFOLIA Michx. Rough Dogwood.

Ma^{n}sa-ĥte-hi (Omaha-Ponca), "real arrow tree" (*ma^{n}sa*, arrow; *ĥte*, real; *hi*, plant body).

Ma^{n}si-hotsh (Winnebago).

Nakipistatu (Pawnee), "real arrow tree" (*nahaapi*, tree; *kipis*, arrow; *tatu*, real).

This was the favorite wood for arrow shafts.

ERICACEAE

UVA-URSI UVA-URSI (L.) Britton. Bearberry.

Nakasis (Pawnee), "little tree," "short tree" (*nakas*, tree; *kasis*, short).

The leaves were used for smoking like tobacco.

OLEACEAE

FRAXINUS PENNSYLVANICA Marsh. Ash.

Pseĥti^n (Dakota).

Tashnánga-hi (Omaha-Ponca).

Rak (Winnebago).

Kiditako (Pawnee).

Ash wood was universally used for making pipestems; it was used also for making bows, and young stems furnished arrow shafts. The ash is one of the trees to which mystic powers are ascribed. J. Owen Dorsey says: "The Omaha have two sacred trees, the ash and the cedar. The ash is connected with the beneficent natural

HERACLEUM LANATUM
Photo by courtesy of George R. Fox, Appleton, Wis.

CORNUS AMOMUM IN BLOOM

b. HABIT OF ASCLEPIAS SYRIACA

Photos by courtesy of Public Museum of Milwaukee, Department of Education

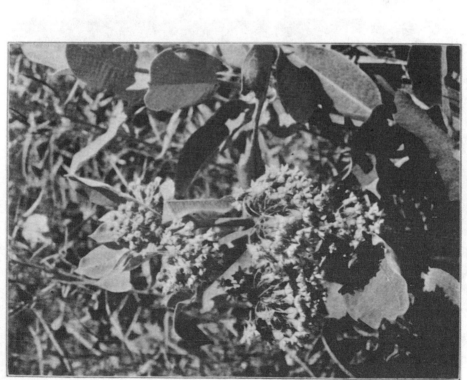

a. ASCLEPIAS SYRIACA, FLOWERS

ASCLEPIAS SYRIACA, FRUITS

powers. Part of the sacred pole of the Omaha and Ponca is made of ash, the other part being of cottonwood." [1]

The stems of the two principal symbolic objects used in the Wawa[n] ceremony of the Omaha and the corresponding ceremony of the Hako of the Pawnee were made of ash wood.

GENTIANACEAE

DASYSTEPHANA PUBERULA (Michx.) Small. Gentian.

Maka[n] chahiwi-cho (Winnebago), "blue-blossom medicine" (*maka[n]*, medicine; *chahiwi*, blossom; *cho*, blue).

Pezhuta-zi (Dakota), "yellow medicine" (*pezhuta*, medicine; *zi*, yellow). So called because of the color of the roots.

A decoction of the root is taken as a tonic; it is so used alone and also in combination with other medicinal plants.

ASCLEPIADACEAE

ASCLEPIAS TUBEROSA L. Butterfly Weed, Pleurisy Root.

Maka[n] saka (Omaha-Ponca), "raw medicine"; (*saka*, raw; *maka[n] saka thata i*, medicine they eat raw). Another name given is *kiu maka[n]*, wound medicine. The name raw medicine was given because this root was used without boiling.

The root was eaten raw for bronchial and pulmonary trouble. It was also chewed and put into wounds, or pulverized when dry and blown into wounds. It was applied as a remedy for old, obstinate sores. In the Omaha tribe this medicine and its rites belonged to the Shell Society. A certain member of the society was the authorized guardian or keeper of this medicine. It was his prerogative to dig the root and distribute bundles of it to the members of the society. The ceremonials connected with the digging, preparation, consecration, and distribution occupied four days. In this connection it may not be out of place to note that four is the dominant number in all ritual and in all orientation in space and time among the Plains tribes, just as the number seven is dominant with some other peoples. Whether four or seven be the dominant number depends on whether the four cardinal points of the horizon are given preeminence or whether equal place is given also to the three remaining points, the Zenith, the Nadir, and the Here.

ASCLEPIAS SYRIACA L. Milkweed. (Pls. 23, 24.)

Wahtha (Omaha-Ponca).

Mahintsh (Winnebago).

Karipiku (Pawnee).

This plant is used for food at three stages of its growth—the young sprouts in early spring, like asparagus sprouts; the clusters

---

[1] Siouan Cults, p. 390.

of floral buds; and the young fruits while firm and green. It is prepared by boiling. Small boys used the fiber of the mature stalks of this plant for popgun wads, chewing it for the purpose.

When the Omaha first saw cabbage and noted its use boiled, as they boiled *waħtha*, they likened it to that, and so named cabbage *waħtha waħe*, "white man's *waħtha*." Likewise the Pawnee named cabbage *karipiku tsahiks-taka*, "white man's *karipiku*" (*tsahiks*, person; *taka*, white).

Asclepias exaltata (L.) Muhl. Tall Milkweed.

> *Waħtha-ska* (Omaha-Ponca), white *waħtha* (*ska*, white; *waħtha*, as stated before, is the Omaha-Ponca name of *Asclepias syriaca*).

The root was eaten raw as a remedy for stomach trouble.

Convolvulaceae

Ipomoea leptophylla Torr. Bush Morning-glory. (Pls. 25, 26.)

> *Kahts-tuwiriki* (Pawnee), "whirlwind medicine" (*tuwiriki*, whirlwind). So called because of the peculiar twisted nature of the fibrovascular system.

Among the Pawnee the large, perennial storage root of this xerophytic plant is highly prized as a remedy for nervousness and bad dreams. For this purpose the smoke treatment was used. For alleviation of pain the pulverized root was dusted on the body with a deer tail or with a feather brush. It was also used to revive one who had fainted.

Cuscuta paradoxa Raf. Dodder, Love Vine.

> *Hakastahkata* (Pawnee), "yellow vine" (*hakastah*, vine; *kata*, yellow).

The dodder vine was used by Pawnee maidens to divine whether their suitors were sincere. A girl having plucked a vine, with the thought of the young man in mind tossed the vine over her shoulder into the weeds of host species of this dodder. Then, turning round, she marked the plant on which the vine fell. The second day after she would return to see whether the dodder had attached itself and was growing on its host. If so, she went away content with full assurance of her lover's sincerity and faithfulness. If the dodder had not twined and attached itself, she took it as a warning not to trust him.

Dodder was said to be used as a dyestuff to give an orange color to feathers. For this purpose the vines were boiled and the materials to be dyed were dipped. A Mexican Indian now living at

IPOMOEA LEPTOPHYLLA (BUSH MORNING-GLORY). AN ENTIRE PLANT,
SHOWING THE LARGE ROOT, ABOUT 4 FEET LONG

Photo by courtesy of Dr. R. J. Pool, University of Nebraska

a. IPOMOEA LEPTOPHYLLA (BUSH MORNING-GLORY), A PERENNIAL FLOWERING
PLANT NATIVE IN THE SAND HILLS OF NEBRASKA, SHOWING HABIT

b. IPOMOEA LEPTOPHYLLA (BUSH MORNING-GLORY)

Photos by courtesy of Dr. R. J. Pool, University of Nebraska

Pine Ridge said his people call it rattlesnake food and say that rattlesnakes take it into their dens for food.

BORAGINACEAE

LITHOSPERMUM CANESCENS (Michx.) Lehm.

Bazu-hi (Omaha-Ponca).

Children used the root of this plant in sport to chew with their gum (gum of *Silphium laciniatum*) to make it of a red color. The flowers of this plant were likewise used to color gum yellow.

VERBENACEAE

VERBENA HASTATA L. Wild Verbena.

Chanhaloga pezhuta (Dakota) ; *pezhuta*, medicine.

Pezhe makan (Omaha-Ponca) ; *pezhe*, herb; *makun*, medicine.

Among the Teton Dakota the leaves were boiled to make a drink as a remedy for stomach ache. Among the Omaha the leaves were steeped merely to make a beverage like tea.

MENTHACEAE

MONARDA FISTULOSA L. Wild Bergamot, Horsemint.

Ḣeḣaka ta pezhuta (Dakota), "elk medicine" (*ḣeḣaka*, elk; *pezhuta*, medicine; *ta*, genitive sign) ; or *ḣeḣaka ta wote*, food of the elk (*wote*, food).

Pezhe pa (Omaha-Ponca), "bitter herb" (*pa*, bitter; *pezhe*, herb).

Tsusahtu (Pawnee), ill smelling.

By the Teton Dakota the flowers and leaves are boiled together to make a medicine which is drunk to cure abdominal pains.

The Winnebago used for pimples and other dermal eruptions on the face an application made by boiling the leaves.

MONARDA FISTULOSA VAR. Washtemna.

Waḣpe washtemna (Dakota), "fragrant leaves" (*waḣpe*, leaf; *washte*, good; *mna*, odorous). This form is one of the plants connected with the Sun dance, according to J. Owen Dorsey.[1]

Izna-kithe-iga hi (Omaha-Ponca), referring to its use in compounding a pomade for the hair. Sometimes called *pezhe-pa minga* in distinction from the other *pezhe-pa*, in reference to its finer essence and more delicate plant body (*minga*, female; female *pezhe-pa*).

Tsostu (Pawnee), meaning, if any, not found.

---

[1] Siouan Cults, p. 454.

In addition to these two forms, the Pawnee, as said before, recognize and name two other forms. All these four forms are included in our taxonomy under the name *Monarda fistulosa*. The two remaining forms, according to the Pawnee classification and nomenclature, are *tsakus tawirat* and *parakaha*. The latter name, *parakaha*, signifies " fragrant "; *tsakus tawirat*, " shot many times still fighting " (*tsakus*, shot many times; *tawirat*, still fighting). In the order of decreasing desirability for fragrance the Pawnee classify the four forms in this order: *parakaha*, *tsakus tawirat*, *tsostu*, and *'tsusahtu*, which last name, meaning ill smelling, shows that it is undesirable, according to their suspectibilities, for this purpose. One or more of the other forms may often be found wherever the last, *tsusahtu*, the common type form of *Monarda fistulosa*, is found. The Pawnee characterize them thus: *tsusahtu*, with stiff strong stems; *tsostu*, with weaker stems and smaller leaves; the next two with weak stems, the most fragrant one, *parakaha*, with stems " as weak as straw." But they also find differences in the roots, and they say these must be compared in order to make identification certain.

The differences noted by the Indians among these varieties, if we may be allowed to call them varieties, are fixed and hereditary and not accidental or dependent on season or situation. Of this I am assured by my own experience with living specimens of the two forms designated by the Dakota *kehaka ta pezhuta* and *wahpe washtemna*. I have transplanted specimens of these two forms from the wild state and have had them under observation at all seasons for five years. I have also noted these two forms in the wild state standing in close proximity to each other.

I give this extended discussion because I have found taxonomists reluctant to admit the possibility of this distinction; at the same time they did not put it to the proof.

HEDEOMA HISPIDA Pursh. Rough Pennyroyal.

Maka chiaka (Dakota).

An infusion of the leaves was used as a remedy for colds. It was used also as a flavor and tonic appetizer in diet for the sick.

MENTHA CANADENSIS L. Wild Mint.

Chiaka (Dakota).

Pezhe nubtho^n (Omaha-Ponca), " fragrant herb " (*nubtho^n*, fragrant).

Kahts-kiwahaaru (Pawnee); " swamp medicine " (*kahts*, from *kahtsu*, medicine; *kiwahaaru*, swamp).

Wild mint was used by all the tribes as a carminative, for this purpose being steeped in water for the patient to drink and sweetened with sugar. Sometimes this infusion was used as a beverage, like tea, not alone for its medicinal property but for its pleasing aromatic flavor.

The Dakota used mint as a flavor in cooking meat. They also packed it with their stores of dried meat, making alternate layers of dried meat and mint.

A Winnebago informant said that traps were boiled with mint in order to deodorize them so that animals might not be deterred by the scent of blood from entering them.

AGASTACHE ANETHIODORA (Nutt.) Britton. Fragrant Giant Hyssop, Wild Anise.

The leaves of this plant were commonly used to make a hot aqueous drink like tea to be taken with meals. It was also used as a sweetening flavor in cookery.

SOLANACEAE

PHYSALIS HETEROPHYLLA Nees. Ground Cherry.

Tamaniokpe (Dakota).

Pe igatush (Omaha-Ponca); *pe*, forehead; *igatush*, to pop. The name has reference to the use by children of the inflated persistent calices which they pop on the forehead in play.

Nikakitspak (Pawnee); *nikako*, forehead; *kitspak*, to pop.

The fruits of the edible species, *P. heterophylla*, are made into a sauce for food by all these tribes. When a sufficient quantity of them was found they were dried for winter. When the Dakota first saw figs they likened them to *Physalis* (*Tamaniokpe*), and called them *Tamaniokpe washichu*[n], "white man's *tamaniokpe*."

PHYSALIS LANCEOLATA Michx.[1] Prairie Ground Cherry.

Maka[n] *bashaho*[n]*-sho*[n] (Omaha-Ponca), "crooked medicine" (*bashasho*[n]*sho*[n], crooked, referring to the root of this species).

Ha[n]*pok-hischasu* (Winnebago), "owl eyes" (*ha*[n]*pok*, owl; *hischasu*, eyes).

The root of this plant was used in the smoke treatment. A decoction of the root was used for stomach trouble and for headache. A dressing for wounds was also made from it.

NICOTIANA QUADRIVALVIS Pursh. Tobacco. (Pl. 27, *b*.)

Cha[n]*di* (Dakota); Teton dialect, *cha*[n]*li*.

Nini-hi (Omaha-Ponca).

This species of *Nicotiana* was cultivated by all the tribes of Nebraska. Since the advent of Europeans tobacco is one of the crops whose culture has been abandoned by these tribes, and they have all lost the seed of it, so that the oldest living Omaha have never seen it growing; but they sometimes receive presents of the prepared tobacco

---

[1] This is the species which is intended by the reference on p. 584 of The Omaha Tribe, *Twenty-seventh Rep. Bur. of Amer. Ethn.* The reference here names *Physalis viscora*, no doubt an error for *P. viscosa*. But *P. viscosa* is native to the Atlantic coast and is not found in the territory of the Omaha.

from other tribes to the north, who are still growing it. From an old man, Long Bear, of the Hidatsa tribe in North Dakota, who was then 73 years old, I obtained specimens and seed in 1908, by which I was able to determine the species. I planted the seed and have had it growing every year since. The plant, when full grown, is only about 60 cm. or 70 cm. in height. It is very hardy and of quick maturity, so that ripe seed will be found in about 60 or 65 days after coming up, and fruit bearing continues till frost comes.

According to Nuttall, *Nicotiana quadrivalvis* was cultivated by all the tribes along the Missouri.[1]

A Pawnee informant said that his people in the old time prepared the ground for planting this tobacco by gathering a quantity of dried grass, which was burned where the patch was to be sown. This kept the ground clear of weeds, so that nothing grew except the tobacco which was planted. The crop was allowed to grow thick, and then the whole plant—leaves, unripe fruit capsules, and the tender, small parts of the stems—was dried for smoking. The unripe seed capsules, dried separately, were specially prized for smoking on account of the flavor, pronounced by the Indians to be like the flavor now found in the imported Turkish tobacco.

A Winnebago informant told me that his people prepared the tobacco by picking off the leaves and laying them out to dry. Next day the partially dry leaves, limp and somewhat viscid, were rolled like tea leaves and again laid to dry. When fully dry the leaves were rubbed fine and stored away. In this finished state the tobacco looks somewhat like gunpowder tea. The Indians said it was of very pleasant odor for smoking. The species of tobacco which was cultivated by the Winnebago, as well as the other tribes of the eastern woodland region, was *Nicotiana rustica* L. It appears that this species was cultivated by all the tribes from the Mississippi River eastward to the Atlantic Ocean. It is said that the woodland tribes eagerly accepted presents of prepared tobacco of the species *Nicotiana quadrivalvis* from the tribes of the plains region and sought to obtain seed of the same, but the plains tribes jealously guarded against allowing the seed to be exported to their woodland neighbors.

Scrophulariaceae

Pentstemon grandiflorus Nutt. Wild Fox-glove.

A Pawnee informant said that he uses this plant as a remedy for chills and fever, but it is not of common knowledge and use. The preparation is a decoction of the leaves, taken internally.

---

[1] Pickering, Chronological History of Plants, p. 741.

a. PEPO FOETIDISSIMA (WILD GOURD) IN BLOOM

b. STRIKES TWO, AN AGED MAN OF THE ARIKARA TRIBE, GATHERING HIS
TOBACCO

PLANTAGINACEAE

PLANTAGO MAJOR L. Plantain.

Sinie maka^n (Omaha-Ponca).

A Ponca gave me the information that a bunch of leaves of this plant made hot and applied to the foot is good to draw out a thorn or splinter.

RUBIACEAE

GALIUM TRIFLORUM Michx. Fragrant Bedstraw, Lady's Bouquet.

Wau-pezhe (Omaha-Ponca), woman's herb, or *wau-inu-maka^n*, woman's perfume (*wau*, woman).

The plant was used by women on account of its fragrance, a delicate odor given off in withering, which resembles the odor of sweetgrass, a handful of the plant being tucked under the girdle.

CAPRIFOLIACEAE

SAMBUCUS CANADENSIS L. Elderberry.

Chaputa (Dakota); *chaputa-hu*, elder bush.

Wagathahashka (Omaha-Ponca); *wagathahashka-hi*, elder bush.

Skirariu (Pawnee).

The fruits were used for food in the fresh state. The larger stems of the bush were used by small boys for making popguns. A pleasant drink was made by dipping the blossoms into hot water.

VIBURNUM LENTAGO L. Black Haw, Nannyberry.

Mna (Dakota); *mna-hu*, black haw bush.

Na^{n}shama^n (Omaha-Ponca).

Wuwu (Winnebago).

Akiwasas (Pawnee); naming names.

The fruits were eaten from the hand, not gathered in quantity.

VIBURNUM OPULUS L. "High-bush Cranberry," Pembina.[1]

In the north, where *Sambucus canadensis* is not found, boys made popguns from stalks of *Viburnum opulus* after removing the pith.

---

[1] The name pembina is herewith proposed as a popular name for this shrub because of the atrocious ineptness of the name "high-bush cranberry," since the berry of *Viburnum* is nothing like a cranberry, and also because of the fact that the name pembina is already commonly applied to this shrub and its fruit by the people of northern North Dakota and Manitoba. The word pembina is a white man's corruption of the name of this berry in the Chippewa language, which is *nepin-minan*, summer-berry; *nepin*, summer; and *minan* berry. The pronunciation of pembina is indicated thus: pĕm'-bĭ-na. This name was applied to a river and mountain in North Dakota, and subsequently to a town and county of that State. The Chippewa call the river *Nepin-minan Sipi* (Summerberry River), because of the abundance of these berries growing along the course of that stream.

They made the piston from a piece of *Amelanchier alnifolia* or of the young growth of *Quercus macrocarpa*. The fibrous inner bark of *Ulmus americana* and of *U. fulva* was used for popgun wads. In the north, where *Betula papyrifera* is found, its papery bark was chewed to a pulp and used for this purpose, while on the western prairie the tops of *Artemisia* were chewed and so used.

SYMPHORICARPOS SYMPHORICARPOS (L.) MacM. Coral Berry, and S. OCCIDENTALIS Hook. Wolf Berry, Buck Brush.

Zuzecha-ta-wote sapsapa (Dakota); black snake food (*zuzecha*, snake; *wote*, food; *ta*, genitive sign; *sapsapa*, reduplication of *sapa*, black).

I^{n}shtogahte-hi (Omaha-Ponca), eye-lotion plant (*i^{n}shta*, eye).

The leaves were steeped to make an infusion used for weak or inflamed eyes.

CUCURBITACEAE

PEPO FOETIDISSIMA (H. B. K.) Britton. Wild Gourd. (Pl. 27, *a*.)

Wagamu^n pezhuta (Dakota), pumpkin medicine (*wagamu^n*, pumpkin; *pezhuta*, medicine).

Niashiga maka^n (Omaha-Ponca), human-being medicine (*niashiga*, human being; *maka^n*, medicine). They say it is male (*niashiga maka^n nuga*) and female (*niashiga maka^n miga*).

This is one of the plants considered to possess special mystic properties. People were afraid to dig it or handle it unauthorized. The properly constituted authorities might dig it, being careful to make the prescribed offering of tobacco to the spirit of the plant, accompanied by the proper prayers, and using extreme care not to wound the root in removing it from the earth. A man of my acquaintance in the Omaha tribe essayed to take up a root of this plant and in doing so cut the side of the root. Not long afterward one of his children fell, injuring its side so that death ensued, which was ascribed by the tribe to the wounding of the root by the father.

This plant is one which is held in particularly high esteem by all the tribes as a medicinal agent. As its range is restricted to the drier parts of the Great Plains, it happens that since the tribes are confined to reservations they can not get it as easily as they did in old times. This explains why, when I have exhibited specimens of the root in seeking information, the Indians have asked for it. While they fear to dig it themselves, after I have assumed the risk of so doing they are willing to profit by my temerity; or it may be that the white man is not held to account by the Higher Powers of the Indian's world.

The root is used medicinally according to the doctrine of signatures, simulating, it is believed, the form of the human body, and

VARIETIES OF SQUASHES AND PUMPKINS CULTIVATED BY TRIBES OF INDIANS OF NEBRASKA FROM IMMEMORIAL TIME

thought to be male and female. As a remedy for any ailment a portion of the root from the part corresponding in position to the affected part of the patient's body is used—for headache or other trouble in the head some of the top of the root is used; for abdominal trouble a bit of the middle of the root; and so on.

A number of species of Cucurbitaceæ were of undoubted aboriginal American culture, as attested by the writings of the earliest explorers, missionaries, and settlers, as well as by the stories, traditions, myths, and religious ceremonies of the various tribes. From all the evidence I have it appears that the tribes of Nebraska prior to European contact certainly cultivated squashes and pumpkins of several varieties, gourds, and possibly watermelons. (Pl. 28.)

When we seek the region in which may possibly be found the original prototypes of the cultivated species grown by the tribes of Nebraska, naturally we must look to the region of the Rio Grande or beyond.

CUCURBITA LAGENARIA L. Dipper Gourd.

Wamnuha or *wakmu* (Dakota).

Peĥe (Omaha-Ponca).

Among the tribes generally the gourd was grown in order to provide shells of which to make rattles. For this purpose the gourd was indispensable, as rattles made therefrom were essential for all ritualistic music. In order to fashion a rattle, the contents of the gourd were removed and a handle was attached. Seeds of *Arisaema triphyllum* or small gravel were placed in the shell.

PEPO PEPO (L.) Pumpkin.

Wamnu (Dakota); Teton dialect, *wagamu*.

Wata (Omaha-Ponca).

Since the advent of Europeans and the consequent disturbance of the aboriginal activities the tribes have lost many of the varieties of their old-time cultivated plants. Some varieties lost by one tribe are still retained by some other tribe, while the latter probably no longer enjoys plants still in possession of the former. Of their old-time squashes the Omaha can describe the following eight varieties, although they have lost the seed of most of them. They do not distinguish between pumpkin and squash, but call them both *wata* with descriptive modifiers affixed. 1. *Wata ĥti*, "real squash" (*ĥti*, real). This term would seem to indicate that this variety has been longest known by the tribe. It is described as being spherical in form, yellowish in color, "like a cottonwood leaf in the fall." 2. *Wata miĥa*, small, spherical, spotted black and green. 3. *Wata nide bazu*, large oval, pointed at the ends, greenish in color. 4. *Wata kukuge*, speckled. 5. *Wata miĥa snede*, long *wata miĥa*.

6. *Wata^n miḱa ska*, white *wata^n miḱa*. 7. *Wata^n miḱa saba*, black *wata^n miḱa*. 8. *Wata^n miḱa zi*, yellow *wata^n miḱa*. These last four squashes, called *wata^n miḱa*, were small summer or fall squashes.

The Omaha planted their squashes at the time of blossoming of the wild plum.

Cucurbita maxima of Tropical or Subtropical America. The *pumpkin* called in Brazilian "jurumu" (Marcgr. 44), in Carib "jujuru" or "babora" (Desc.), and cultivated from early times: "pompions" were seen by Columbus in 1493 on Guadalope (F. Columb. 47) . . . C. maxima was observed by De Soto in 1542 in Florida, and is known to have been cultivated by the North American tribes as far as the St. Lawrence.[1]

April 12, 1528 (Cabeza de Vaca, and Churchill Coll.), arrival of exped. of Pamphilo de Narvaez on north side of Gulf of Mexico, west of Mississippi R. Landed, proceeded inland, and observed pumpkins and beans cultivated by the natives.[2]

About their howses they have commonly square plotts of cleered grownd, which serve them for gardens, some one hundred, some two hundred foote square, wherein they sowe their tobacco, pumpons, and a fruit like unto a musk million, but lesse and worse, which they call macock gourds, and such like, which fruicts increase exceedingly, and ripen in the beginning of July, and contynue untill September; they plant also the field apple, the maracock, a wyld fruit like a kind of pomegranett, which increaseth infinitlye, and ripens in August, contynuing untill the end of October, when all the other fruicts be gathered, but they sowe nether herb, flower, nor any other kynd of fruict.[3]

PEPO MAXIMA (Duch.) Peterm. Squash.

This species is found in tropical and subtropical North America.

The *squash*; called by the New England tribes "*askutasquash*" (R. Will.), and cultivated from early times:—observed under cultivation by the natives by W. Wood, R. Williams, and Josselyn; is known to have been cultivated throughout our middle and southern States; by the natives in the West Indies, as appears from Dalechamp pl. 616, and was seen by Chanvalon on Martinique (Poiret dict. nat. XI, 234.)[4]

To the southwest, whence came the crop plants of aboriginal culture in Nebraska, the remains in ruins sometimes reveal the identity of plants of ancient culture there.

The occurrence of squash seeds in some of the mortuary bowls is important, indicating the ancient use of this vegetable for food. It may, in this connection, be borne in mind that one of the southern clans of the Hopi Indians was called the Patuñ or Squash family.[5]

Pepo pepo, Dr. J. H. Coulter says, "Has a naturalized variety in southern and western Texas, ... (*C. texana* Gray)."[6]

---

[1] Pickering, Chronological History of Plants, pp. 709–710.
[2] Ibid., p. 869.
[3] William Strachey, Historie of Travaile into Virginia Britannia, p. 72 (1612).
[4] Pickering, op. cit., p. 747.
[5] Fewkes, Two Summers' Work in Pueblo Ruins, p. 101.
[6] Coulter, Botany of Western Texas, p. 124.

Pumpkin seeds have been found in old Pawnee graves in Nebraska. The squash is mentioned in the Onondaga creation myth, showing that it has been in cultivation by that tribe from ancient times, and this is evidence of its wide distribution from the area of its origin.[1]

Religious expression is one of the most conservative elements and does not readily take up any new thing, hence the religious songs of a people indicate those things which have been for a long time familiar to that people. Allusion is made to the squash in some of the oldest religious songs of the Pima tribe in the southwest. One of the most ancient hymns to bring rain is the following.

> Hi-ilo-o ya-a-a ! He the All-seeing
> Sees the two stalks of corn standing;
> He's my younger brother. Hi-ilo-o ya-a-a !
> He the All-seeing sees the two squashes ;
> He's my younger brother. Hi-ilo-o ya-a-a !
> On the summit of Ta-atukam sees the corn standing;
> He's my younger brother. Hi-ilo-o ya-a-a !
> On the summit of Ta-atukam sees the squash standing;
> He's my younger brother. Hi-ilo-o woiha !

Another Pima rain song:

> Hi-ihiya naiho-o ! The blue light of evening
> Falls as we sing before the sacred âmĭna.
> About us on all sides corn tassels are waving.
> Hitciya yahina ! The white light or day dawn
> Yet finds us singing, while corn tassels are waving.
> Hitciya yahina-a ! The blue light of evening
> Falls as we sing before the sacred âmĭna.
> About us on all sides corn tassels are waving.
> Hitciya yahina ! The white light of day dawn
> Yet finds us singing, while the squash leaves are waving.[2]

CUCURBITA FICIFOLIA Bouché. (*C. melanosperma*, A. Br.)

The specimens correspond closely with the description of this species (hitherto known only as cultivated in European gardens and conjectured to be from the East Indies) excepting in the shape of the leaves, which have the lobes (often short) and sinuses acute instead of rounded. Guadalajara, cultivated; September (620).—The fruit, called " cidra cayote " or " chila cayote," is about a foot in length, resembling a watermelon in appearance, with a hard outer shell, the contents white and fibrous, and seeds black. It keeps for many months without decay. A preserve is made of the inner fibrous portion. The name " cayote," given to this and other cucurbitaceous species in Mexico, may be the equivalent of the " chayote " of Cervantes and the " chayotli " of Hernandez.[3]

---

[1] Hewitt, Iroquoian Cosmology, p. 174.
[2] Russell, The Pima Indians, p 332.
[3] Watson, Contributions to American Botany, p. 414.

CITRULLUS CITRULLUS (L.) Karst.   Watermelon.   (Pls. 29, 29A.)

   Saka yutapi (Dakota), Santee dialect, eaten raw (*saka*, raw);
     Yankton and Teton dialect, *shpaⁿshni yutapi*, eaten uncooked
     (*shpaⁿshni*, uncooked).
   Saka thide (Omaha-Ponca), or *saka thata*, eaten raw (*saka*, raw).
   Wathaka ratdshe (Oto).

When I first inquired of the Omaha in regard to their ancient cultivated crops, they named watermelons as one of the crops grown from time immemorial. They said they had a kind of watermelon which was small, round, and green, having a thin rind and red flesh, with small, black, shining seeds; that it was different from the melons now grown from seed introduced since the coming of white men. I read the statement made by an early explorer coming up the Missouri River that the Oto brought presents of watermelons to the boat. I received from the Ponca, the Pawnee, and the Cheyenne an account which was perfectly uniform with that I had from the Omaha, even to the gestural description of the melon. Lastly, I was told by a white man who was born in northern Texas and had been familiar all his life with the natural characteristics of northern Texas and southern Oklahoma, that he had often found and eaten wild watermelons on the sand bars and banks of Red River, Pecos River, and other streams of northwestern Texas. He said further that his father had told him of finding them on still other streams of that region. This man described the wild watermelons to me exactly as all the tribes before mentioned had described their cultivated melons.

This hitherto unthought of probability of the presence on the American continent of an indigenous species of *Citrullus* caused me to make search through the literature and to make inquiry by correspondence, with the results I have here appended. The more I searched into the matter the more unlikely it seemed to me that even so desirable a fruit as the watermelon, should it be granted to have been introduced by the Spaniards at the time of their very first settlement, could have been disseminated with such astonishing rapidity and thoroughness as to be found so common among so many tribes of eastern North America from the Gulf of Mexico to the Great Lakes, and from the Atlantic coast to the Great Plains. Such a result would be all the more astonishing, considering the barriers to be passed in its passage from tribe to tribe; barriers of racial antagonism, of diverse languages, of climatic adaptation, and the ever-present barrier of conservatism, of unwillingness of any people to adopt a new thing. But if none of these barriers had intervened, and if each tribe had zealously propagated and distributed as rapidly as possible to its neighbors, it can scarcely be believed that time

a. STAMINATE AND PISTILLATE FLOWERS OF WATERMELON GROWN FROM
SEED OBTAINED FROM PENISHKA, AN OLD MAN OF THE PONCA TRIBE

b. UNIT OF VINE OF ABOVE

Photos by courtesy of W. E. Safford, U. S. Department of Agriculture

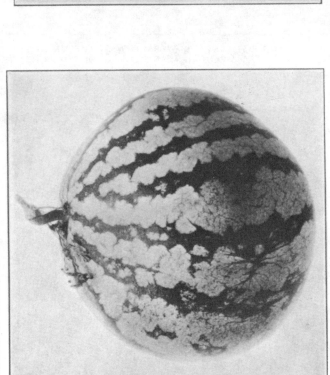

WATERMELON GROWN FROM SEED OBTAINED FROM PENISHKA, AN OLD MAN OF THE PONCA TRIBE

Photos by courtesy of W. E. Safford, U. S. Department of Agriculture

enough had elapsed for this to be accomplished at the first contact of the French and English explorers. The watermelons grown by the various tribes seem to be of a variety distinct from any of the many known varieties of European introduction.

I append here some quotations from literature which I have found in various sources bearing on the subject.

J. M. Coulter (Cont. U. S. Nat. Herb., vol. II, p. 123, Botany of Western Texas), after describing adds: " Said by Dr. Havard to be found wild in many places west of the Pecos."

Concerning its origin, C. Conzatti, in " Los Géneros Vegetales Mexicanos," p. 348, states:

. . . Es género introducido del Viejo Mundo, y de él se cultiva entre nosotros una de las dos especies que comprende: *C. vulgaris* Schrad., ó " Cidracayote." [1]

According to De Bry the watermelon is—

Une plante dont l'origine est incertaine d'après les auteurs. Linné (*Sp.*, p. 1435) dit: " Habitat in Apulia, Calabria, Sicilia." Seringe (*Prodr.*, III, p. 301) dit: " in Africa et India." Puis il ajoute une variété décrite au Brésil par Marcgraf, ce qui complique encore la question. . . .

La planche et le texte de Marcgraf (*Bras.*, p. 22) me paraissent bien s'appliquer à la Pastèque. D'un autre côté, rien ne prouve que la plante n'eût pas été apportée au Brésil pas les Européens, si ce n'est le fait d'un nom vulgaire *Jaee*, mais l'argument n'est pas fort. Marcgraf cite aussi des noms européens. Il ne dit pas que l'espèce fût spontanée, ni très généralement cultivée. Sloane l'indique comme cultivée à la Jamaïque (I, p. 226), sans prétendre q'elle fût américaine, et assurément le silence des premiers auteurs, sauf Marcgraf, le rend bien peu probable. [2]

Je conclus de ce qui précède que toutes les espèces de *Citrullus* énumérées dans la synonymie que j'ai donnée ci-dessus n'en font qu'une; que cette espèce, toujours annuelle, et par là facile à distinguer de la Coloquinte officinale, est essentiellement africaine; qu'elle existe encore à l'état sauvage en Afrique, et qu'elle est cultivée depuis un temps immémorial dans la vallée du Nil, d'où elle a passé, même anciennement, chez la plupart des peuples civilises du bassin méditerranéen Aujourd'hui, elle existe dans tous les pay chauds de la terre, et comme les graines en sont jetées au hasard, partout où on la consomme, il n'y a rien, d'étonnant qu'on la retrouve à demi-sauvage dans beaucoup de contrées où elle n'existait certainement pas primitivement. [3]

Saka¢ide uke¢iⁿ, the common watermelon, was known to the Omahas before the coming of the white men. It has a green rind, which is generally striped, and the seeds are black. It is never dried, but is always eaten raw, hence the name. They had no yellow saka¢ide till the whites came; but they do not eat them. [4]

The Mahas [Omahas] seem very friendly to the whites, and cultivate corn, beans, melons, squashes, and a small species of tobacco [Nicotiana quadrivalvis]. [5]

---

[1] Conzatti, Los Géneros Vegetales Mexicanos, p. 348.
[2] De Candolle, Geographie Botanique, Tome 2, p. 908.
[3] Naudin, Revue des Cucurbitacées, Annales des Sciences Naturelles, 4ᵉ Serie, Tome XII, pp. 107–108.
[4] Dorsey, Omaha Sociology, p. 306.
[5] Bradbury, Travels in the Interior of America, p. 77.

Watermelons are cultivated in great plenty in the English and French-American colonies, and there is hardly a peasant here who has not a field planted with them. . . . The Indians plant great quantities of watermelons at present, but whether they have done it of old is not easily determined. For an old Onidoe Indian (of the six Iroquese Nations) assured me that the Indians did not know watermelons before the Europeans came into the country and communicated them to the Indians. The French, on the other hand, have assured me that the Illinois Indians have had abundance of this fruit, when the French first came to them, and that they declare, they had planted them since times immemorial. However, I do not remember having read that the Europeans, who first came to North America, mention the watermelons in speaking of the dishes of the Indians of that time.[1]

After several miles of marching along extensive and well-cultivated fields of squashes, pumpkins, beans, melons, and corn the Dragoons reached the village.

Here then was the Toyash or Pawnee Pict village, the main goal of this expedition. . . . Col. Dodge encamped in a fine position about a mile from the village, and the hungry Dragoons were soon enjoying the Indian hospitalities. Dishes of corn and beans dressed with buffalo fat were placed before them. For dessert the soldiers enjoyed liberal supplies of watermelons and wild plums.[2]

When Garces was among the Yumas in 1775 they were raising "countless" calabashes and melons—*calabazas y melones*—perhaps better translated squashes and cantaloupes, or pumpkins and muskmelons. The Piman and Yuman tribes cultivated a full assortment of cucurbitaceous plants, not always easy to identify by their old Spanish names. The *Sandía* was the watermelon invariably; the *melon*, usually a muskmelon, or cantaloupe; the *calabaza*, a calabash, gourd, pumpkin, or squash of some sort, including one large, rough kind like our crook-neck squash."[3]

MELONS AMONG THE NATCHEZ

Father Petit in a letter to Father d'Avauguor, from New Orleans, July 12, 1730, writes, "Each year the people assemble to plant one vast field with Indian corn, beans, pumpkins, and melons, and then again they collect in the same way to gather the harvest."[4]

The vegetables they [the Iroquois] cultivate most are Maize, or Turkey corn, French beans, gourds, and melons. They have a sort of gourd smaller than ours, and which taste much of sugar [squashes]; they boil them whole in water, or roast them under the ashes, and so eat them without any other preparation. The Indians were acquainted, before our arrival in their country, with the common and water melon.[5]

Toute sorte de Melons croissent à souhait dans la Louisiane; ceux d'Espagne, de France, et les melons Anglois, que l'on nomme melons blancs, y son infiniment meilleurs que dans les Pays dont ils portent le nom: mais les plus excellens de tous sont les melons d'eau. Comme ils sont peu connus en France, où l'on n'en voit guéres que dans la Provence, encore sont-ils de la petite espèce, je crois que l'on ne donne trouvera point mauvais que j'en la description.

---

1 Kalm, Travels into North America, vol. 2, p. 385.
2 Pelzer, Henry Dodge, p. 100.
3 Russell, The Pima Indians, p. 91.
4 *Jesuit Relations,* vol. 68, p. 137.
5 Charlevoix, Journal of a Voyage to North America, vol. I, p. 250.

La tige de ce melon rampe comme celle des nôtres, et s'étend jusqu'à dix pieds de l'endroit d'où elle sort de terre. Elle est si délicate, que lorsqu'on l'écrase en marchant dessus, le fruit meurt; et pour peu qu'on la froisse, il s'échaude. Les feuilles sont très découpées, d'un verd qui tire sur le verd de mer, et larges comme la main quand elles sont ouvertes. Le fruit est ou rond comme les potirons, ou long: il se trouve de bons melons de cotte dernière espèce; mais ceux de la première espèce sont plus estimés, et meritent de l'être. Le poids des plus gros passe rarement trente livres; mais celui des plus petits est toujours au dessus de dix livres. Leur côte et d'un verd pâle, mêlé de grandes taches blanches, et la chair qui touche à cette côte est blanche, crue, et d'une verdeur désagréable; aussi ne la mange t-on jamais. L'intérieur est rempli par une substance légere et brillante comme une neige, qui seroit de couleur de rose: elle fond dans la bouche comme seroit la neige même, et laisse un goût pareil à clui de cette eau que l'on prépare pour les malades avec de la gelée de groseille. Ce fruit ne peut donc être que très rafraîchissant, et il est si sain que de quelque maladie que l'on soit attaqué, on peut en satisfaire son appétit sans crainte d'en être incommodé. Les melons d'eau d'Afrique ne sont point à beaucoup près si délicieux que ceux de la Louisiane.

La graine du melon d'eau est placée comme celle du melon de France; sa figure est ovale, plate, aussi épaisse à ses extrémités que vers son centre, et à environs six lignes de long sur quatre de large: les unes l'ont noire et les autres rouge; mais la noire est la meilleure, et c'est celle qu'il convient de sémer pour être assuré d'avoir de bons fruits, pourvû qu'on ne la mette pas dans des terres fortes, où elle dégénéreroit et deviendroit rouge.[1]

TRANSLATION

All kinds of melons grow admirably well in Louisiana. Those of Spain, of France, of England, which last are called white melons, are there infinitely finer than in the countries from which they have their name; but the best of all are the watermelons. As they are hardly known in France, except in Provence, where a few of the small kind grow, I fancy a description of them will not be disagreeable to the reader.

The stalk of this melon spreads like ours upon the ground, and extends to the length of ten feet. It is so tender that when it is in any way bruised by treading upon it the fruit dies; and if it is rubbed in the least it is scorched. The leaves are very much divided, as broad as the hand when they are spread out, and are somewhat of a sea-green colour. The fruit is either round like a pompion, or long. There are some good melons of this last kind, but the first sort are the most esteemed and deservedly so. The weight of the largest rarely exceeds thirty pounds, but that of the smallest is always about ten pounds. Their rind is of a pale green colour, interspersed with large white spots. The substance that adheres to the rind is white, crude, and of a disagreeable tartness, and is therefore never eaten. The space within that is filled with a light and sparkling substance, that may be called for its properties a rose-coloured snow. It melts in the mouth as if it were actually snow, and leaves a taste like that of the water prepared for sick people from currant jelly. This fruit cannot fail, therefore, of being very refreshing, and is so wholesome that persons in all kinds of distempers may satisfy their appetite with it, without any apprehension of being the worse for it. The watermelons of Africa are not near so refreshing as those of Louisiana.

---

[1] Le Page du Pratz, Histoire de la Louisiane, Tome 2, pp. 12–14.

The seeds of watermelons are like those of French melons. Their shape is oval and flat, being as thick at the ends as towards the middle; their length is about six lines, and their breadth four. Some are black and others red; but the black are the best, and it is those you ought to chuse for sowing, if you would wish to have the best fruit; which you can not fail of if they are not planted in strong ground where they would degenerate and become red.

MELONS GROWN BY INDIANS OF VIRGINIA BEFORE THE COMING OF WHITE MEN

. . . but none of the Toils of Husbandry were exercised by this happy People, except the bare planting a little Corn and Melons, . . . And indeed all that the *English* have done since their going thither, has been only to make some of these Native Pleasures more scarce. . . . hardly making Improvements equivalent to that Damage.[1]

MELONS FOUND BY LA SALLE IN TEXAS IN 1687

This instrument [wooden hoe] serves them instead of a hoe, or spade, for they have no iron tools. When the land has been thus tilled, or broken up, the women sow and plant the Indian corn, beans, pompions, watermelons and other grain and garden ware, which is for their sustenance. [Account of the Cenis, (Caddos), 1687.][2]

. . . we met a company of Indians, with axes, going to fetch barks of trees to cover their cottages. They were surprised to see us, but having made signs to them to draw near, they came, caressed and presented us with some watermelons they had . . . We halted in one of their cottages, . . . There we met several women who had brought bread, gourds, beans and watermelons, a sort of fruit proper to quench thirst, the pulp of it being no better than water.[3]

WATERMELONS AMONG THE ILLINOIS

We continued some time in Fort Louis [on the Mississippi among the Illinois] without receiving any news. Our business was, after having heard mass, which we had the good fortune to do every day, to divert ourselves the best way we could. The Indian women daily brought in something fresh; we wanted not for watermelons, bread made of Indian corn, baked in the embers, and other such things, and we rewarded them by little presents in return.[4]

The natives of the country about (among the Poutouatannis [Pottawatomies] which is half way to Michilimaquinay) till the land and sow Indian corn, melons and gourds.[5]

MELONS AND OTHER CULTIVATED PLANTS AMONG TRIBES OF WESTERN PRAIRIES

The savage peoples who inhabit the prairies have life-long good-fortune; animals and birds are found there in great numbers, with numberless rivers abounding in fish. Those people are naturally very industrious, and devote

---

[1] Beverley, History of Virginia (1705), Book II, p. 40.
[2] Cox, Journeys of La Salle, vol. II, p. 139.
[3] Ibid., pp. 190–191.
[4] Ibid., p. 222.
[5] Ibid., p. 229.

themselves to the cultivation of the soil, which is very fertile for Indian corn. It produces also beans, squashes (both small and large) of excellent flavor, fruits, and many kinds of roots. They have in especial a certain method of preparing squashes with the Indian corn cooked while in its milk, which they mix and cook together and then dry, a food which has a very sweet taste. Finally, melons grow there which have a juice no less agreeable than refreshing.[1]

The relation of Marquette's first voyage, 1673–1677, mentions " melons, which are excellent, especially those that have red seeds," among the Illinois.[2]

Thence we ascended to Montreal. . . . The latitude is about that of Bordeaux, but the climate is very agreeable. The soil is excellent, and if the Gardener but throw some Melon seeds on a bit of loosened earth among the stones they are sure to grow without any attention on his part. Squashes are raised there with still greater ease, but differ much from ours—some of them having when cooked, almost the taste of apples or of pears.[3]

WATERMELONS AMONG CULTIVATED CROPS OF VIRGINIA INDIANS

Several Kinds of the Creeping Vines bearing Fruit, the *Indians* planted in their Gardens or Fields, because they would have Plenty of them always at hand ; such as Musk-melons, Watermelons, Pompions, Cushaws, Macocks and Gourds.

1. Their Musk-melons resemble the large *Italian* Kind, and generally fill Four or Five Quarts.

2. Their Water-melons were much more large, and of several Kinds, distinguished by the Colour of their Meat and Seed ; some are red, some yellow, and others white meated ; and so of the Seed ; some are yellow, some red, and some black ; but these are never of different colours in the same Melon. This Fruit the *Muscovites* call *Arpus;* the *Turks* and *Tartars Karpus*, because they are extremely cooling: The *Persians* call them *Hindannes*, because they had the first Seed of them from the *Indies*. They are excellently good, and very pleasant to the Taste, as also to the Eye; having the Rind of a lively green colour, streak'd and water'd, the Meat of a Carnation and the Seed black and shining, while it lies in the Melon.

3. Their Pompions I need not describe, but must say they are much larger and finer, than any I ever heard of in England.

4. Their *Cushaws* are a kind of Pompion, of a bluish green colour, streaked with White, when they are fit for Use. They are larger than the Pompions, and have a long, narrow Neck. Perhaps this may be the *Ecushaw* of *T. Harriot.*

5. Their *Macocks* are a sort of *Melopepones*, or lesser sort of Pompion or cushaw. Of these they have great Variety; but the *Indian* Name *Macock* serves for all, which Name is still retain'd among them. Yet the *Clypeatæ* are sometimes called *Cymnels*, (as are some others also) from the *Lenten* Cake of that Name, which many of them very much resemble. *Squash*, or *Squanter-Squash*, is their Name among the Northern *Indians,* and so they are call'd in *New-York* and *New-England.* These being boil'd whole, when the Apple is young, and the Shell tender, and dished with Cream or Butter, relish very

---

[1] Perrot, Mémoire, in Blair, Indians of the Upper Mississippi, vol. I, p. 113. (Written probably during 1680 to 1718.)

[2] *Jesuit Relations*, vol. 59, p. 129.

[3] Relation of 1662–1663, in *Jesuit Relations*, vol. 48, p. 169.

well with all sorts of Butcher's Meat, either fresh or salt. And whereas the Pompion is never eaten till it be ripe, these are never eaten after they are ripe.

6. The *Indians* never eat the Gourds, but plant them for other uses . . . [They] use the Shells, instead of Flagons and Cups. . . .

7. The *Maracock*, which is the Fruit of what we call the Passion-Flower, our Natives did not take the Pains to plant, having enough of it growing everywhere; tho' they eat it . . . this Fruit is about the Size of a Pullet's Egg.

Besides all these, our Natives had originally amongst them, *Indian* Corn, Peas, Beans, Potatoes, and Tobacco. This *Indian* Corn was the Staff of Food, upon which the *Indians* did ever depend. . . .

There are Four Sorts of *Indian* Corn: Two of which are early ripe, and Two, late ripe, all growing in the same manner; every single Grain of this when planted, produces a tall, upright Stalk, which has several Ears hanging on the Sides of it, from Six to Ten Inches long. Each Ear is wrapt up in a Cover of many Folds, to protect it from the Injuries of the Weather. In every one of these Ears are several rows of Grain, set close to one another, with no other Partition, but a very thin Husk. So that oftentimes the Increase of this Grain amounts to above a Thousand for one.

The Two Sorts which are early ripe, are distinguish'd only by the Size, which shows itself as well in the Grain as in the Ear and the Stalk. There is some Difference also in the Time of ripening.

The lesser Size of Early ripe Corn yields an Ear not much larger than the Handle of a Case Knife, and grows upon a Stalk between Three and Four Feet high. Of this are commonly made Two Crops in a Year, and, perhaps, there might be Heat enough in *England* to ripen it.

The larger Sort differs from the former only in Largeness, the Ear of this being Seven or Eight Inches long, as thick as a Child's Leg, and growing upon a Stalk Nine or Ten feet high. This is fit for eating about the latter End of May, whereas the smaller Sort (generally speaking) affords Ears fit to roast by the middle of May. The grains of both these Sorts are as plump and swell'd as if the Skin were ready to burst.

The late ripe Corn is diversify'd by the Shape of the Grain only, without any Respect to the accidental Differences in colour, some being blue, some red, some yellow, some white, and some streak'd. That therefore which makes the Distinction, is the Plumpness or Shriveling of the Grain; the one looks as smooth, and as full as the early ripe Corn, and this they call *Flint-Corn;* the other has a larger grain, and looks shrivell'd, with a Dent on the Back of the Grain, as if it had never come to Perfection; and this they call *She-Corn*. This is esteem'd by the Planters as the best for Increase, and is universally chosen by them for planting; yet I can't see but that this also produces the Flint-Corn, accidentally among the other.

All these Sorts are planted alike, in Rows, Three, Four or Five Grains in a Hill; the larger sort at Four or Five feet Distance, the lesser Sort nearer. The *Indians* used to give it One or Two Weedings, and make a Hill about it, and so the labour was done. They likewise plant a Bean in the same Hill with the Corn, upon whose Stalk it sustains itself.

The *Indians* sow'd Peas sometimes in the Intervals of the Rows of Corn, but more generally in a Patch of Ground by themselves. They have an unknown Variety of them (but all of a Kidney-Shape), some of which I have met with wild; but whence they had their *Indian* Corn I can give no Account; for I don't believe that it was spontaneous in those parts.

Their Potatoes are either red or white, about as long as a Boy's Leg, and sometimes as long and as big as both the Leg and Thigh of a young Child, and very much resembling it in Shape. I take these Kinds to be the same with those, which are represented in the Herbals to be *Spanish* Potatoes. I am sure, those call'd *English* or *Irish* Potatoes are nothing like these, either in Shape, Colour, or Taste. The Way of progagating Potatoes there, is by cutting the small ones to Pieces, and planting the Cuttings in Hills of loose Earth; but they are so tender, that it is very difficult to preserve them in the Winter, for the least Frost coming at them, rots and destroys them, and therefore People bury 'em under Ground, near the Fire-Hearth all the Winter until the Time comes, that their Seedings are to be set.

How the *Indians* order'd their Tobacco I am not certain, they now depending chiefly upon the *English* for what they smoak; but I am inform'd they used to let it all run to Seed, only succouring the Leaves to keep the Sprouts from growing upon, and starving them; and when it was ripe, they pull'd off the Leaves, cured them in the Sun, and laid them up for Use. But the Planters make a heavy Bustle with it now, and can't please the Market neither.[1]

CULTIVATED CROPS, INDIANS OF VIRGINIA; MELONS

Pagatowr a kind of graine so called by the inhabitants; the same in the West Indies is called Mayze; Englishmen call it Guinney-wheate or Turkie wheate, according to the names of the countrey from whence the like hath been brought. The graine is about the bignesse of our ordinary English peaze and not much different in forme and shape: but of divers colours: some white, some red, some yellow and some blew. All of them yeelde a very white and sweete flowre being according to his kinde, at maketh a very good bread. Wee made of the same in the countrey some mault, whereof was brued as good ale as was to bee desired. So likewise by the help of hops thereof may bee made as good Beere. . . .

Okindgier, called by us beanes, because in greatnesse and partly in shape they are like to the Beanes of England, saving that they are flatter. . . .

Wickonzowr, called by us peaze, in respect of the beanes for distinction sake, because they are much lesse; although in forme they little differ. . . .

Macocqwer, according to their severall formes, called by us, Pompions, Mellions, and Gourdes, because they are of the like formes as those kindes in England.[2]

I have also seen, once, a plant similar to the Melon of India, with fruit the size of a small lime.[3]

He does not state at what stage of growth he saw it "the size of a small lime." He mentions pumpkins in the same *Relation*.

They [the Illinois Indians as seen by him on his first visit] "live by game, which is abundant in this country, and on Indian corn [bled d'inde], of which they always gather a good crop, so that they have never suffered by famine. They also sow beans and melons, which are excellent, especially those with a red seed. Their squashes are not of the best; they dry them in the sun to eat in the winter and spring.[4]

---

[1] Beverley, History of Virginia, Book II, p. 26 et seq.
[2] Hariot, A Briefe and True Report, pp. 13–14.
[3] Bressani's Relation, 1652–1653, in *Jesuit Relations*, vol. 38, p. 243.
[4] Narrative of Father Marquette, in French, *Historical Collections of Louisiana*, pt. IV, p. 33.

DESCRIPTION OF DOMESTIC LIFE OF VIRGINIA INDIANS IN 1585; MENTION
OF MELONS.

From De Bry:

" Some of their towns . . . are not inclosed with a palisade, and are much
more pleasant; Secotan, for example, here drawn from nature. The houses
are more scattered, and a greater degree of comfort and cultivation is observed, with gardens in which tobacco . . . is cultivated, woods filled with
deer, and fields of corn. In the fields they erect a stage . . . in which a
sentry is stationed to guard against the depredations of birds and thieves.
Their corn they plant in rows . . . , for it grows so large, with thick stalk
and broad leaves, that one plant would stint the other and it would never
arrive at maturity. They have also a curious place . . . where they convene
with their neighbors at their feasts, . . . and from which they go to the feast.
On the opposite side is their place of prayer . . . , and near to it the sepulcher
of their chiefs . . . They have gardens for melons . . . and a place . . . where
they build their sacred fires. At a little distance from the town is the pond
. . . from which they obtain water." [1]

In the light of what I had heard from the Indians and what I
found in the writings of the first white men who came in contact
with the tribes, I wrote to several persons, whose replies follow; these
are self-explanatory.

. . . As to Shawnees raising watermelons before the advent of our white
brethren, I doubt it; I have never heard of their raising any melons except
those whose seed was first given them by the early Jesuit fathers when they
lived on the Wapakoneta in Ohio. However, they did raise a small pumpkin,
which they called by a name meaning " little pumpkin," from which I deduce
that they probably raised a larger variety, but of which they seem to have lost
the seed.

DECEMBER 4, 1914.   PIERREPONT ALFORD,
                                                       Econtuchka, Okla.

I regret that I can not give you anything worth while about watermelons in
North America. I have met the plant throughout the eastern United States,
particularly in the Southern States, but only as an escape.

JANUARY 12, 1914.   J. K. SMALL,
                                                New York Botanic Garden,
                                               Bronx Park, New York City.

We have the small round melon with the small black seed. We sell it under
the name of the Pickaninny. . . . I don't know anything about the origin of
this variety; we got it from a woman in Kansas.

JANUARY 13, 1914.   HENRY FIELD SEED CO.,
                                             By HENRY FIELD, *President.*

We have your favor of the 8th instant, and in reply mail you a copy of
Burpee's Annual for 1914, and for small fruited variety of watermelon refer
you to the Baby Delight, described on page 21. We also have offered for
several seasons seed of Burpee's Hungarian Honey watermelon, which is early,

---

[1] De Bry, quoted by Thomas, Mound Explorations, p. 622.

small in size, and has deep-red flesh of finest quality. . . . The seed of Baby
Delight, you will note, is not black, but of a light brown. . . .

JANUARY 14, 1914.   W. ATLEE BURPEE & Co.,
                                                        Philadelphia, Pa.

Your letter received. I did not answer at once because I wished to confer
with Prof. Thoburn, who has been absent from the university investigating
some mounds supposed to be of historical interest.

He agrees with me that the watermelons to which you refer in your letter
are what are popularly known as the "volunteer melon." I have a ranch in
an Indian neighborhood and the so-called "pie melon" or citron is almost a
pest. The "volunteer melons" are not unusual and they often hybridize
with the "pie melon." This may account for the fact that the "volunteer
melon" differs from the ordinary melon of commerce. While I have no proof
to sustain my statement, I do not believe that the melon is indigenous to
Oklahoma.

Should there develop any further information in regard to the subject I
shall be glad to communicate with you further. I shall be much interested
in the results of your investigation and hope to keep in touch with the work
which you are doing in this line.

JANUARY 23, 1914.   A. H. VAN VLEET,
                               Professor of Biology and Dean of the Graduate
                                  School, the University of Oklahoma.

MICRAMPELIS LOBATA (Michx.) Greene. Wild Cucumber.

Waknaknahecha (Dakota).

Wataⁿgtha (Omaha-Ponca), from *wataⁿ*, squash or melon, and
iⁿgtha, ghost; ghost melon.

An Oglala said the seeds were used for beads.

CAMPANULACEAE

LOBELIA CARDINALIS L. Red Lobelia, Cardinal Flower, Red Betty.

This species is peculiar in its situation in Nebraska, in that it is
found in some isolated areas, all within the ancient domain of the
Pawnee Nation. These areas are far distant from any other region
in which the species is found. It is listed among "Species peculiar
to the Republican District."[1] Again "*Lobelia cardinalis* and *L.
inflata,* which are known for one or two stations in III [Sand Hill
region] along the southern edge of the State."[2]

In another part of the present work the suggestion is made that
the presence of this species in the Pawnee country may be due to
introduction by Pawnee medicine-men. This explanation is suggested in view of the value placed on the mystic powers attributed
to the species by that people. One use of this plant was in the
composition of a love charm. The roots and flowers were the parts
used. Other plants combined with *Lobelia* in compounding this
charm were roots of *Panax quinquefolium* and *Angelica*[3] and the
seed of *Cogswellia daucifolia.*

---

[1] Clements and Pound, Phytogeography of Nebraska, p. 81.

[2] Ibid, p. 297.

[3] See discussion of *Panax.*

COMPOSITAE

HELIANTHUS ANNUUS L. Sunflower.

Wakcha-zizi (Dakota), "yellow flower" (*wakcha*, flower; *zizi*, reduplication of *zi*, yellow).

Zha-zi (Omaha-Ponca), "yellow weed" (*zha*, weed; *zi*, yellow).

Kirik-tara-kata (Pawnee), "yellow-eyes" (*kirik*, eye; *tara*. having; *kata*, yellow).

I can not find that the sunflower was ever cultivated by any of the Nebraska tribes, although its culture among eastern tribes is reported by explorers, and it was and still is cultivated by the Arikara, Mandan, and Hidatsa in North Dakota. P. de Charlevoix, in a letter written in April, 1721, mentions sunflowers as one of the crops of the tribes of eastern Canada.

The *soleil* is another very common plant in the fields of the Indians, and which rises to the height of seven or eight feet. Its flower, which is very thick, has much the same figure with that of the marigold, and the seed is disposed in the same manner; the Indians extract an oil from it by boiling, with which they anoint their hair. [1]

Champlain observed the sunflower cultivated by Indians in Canada in 1615. [2]

All the country where I went [vicinity of Lake Simcoe, Ontario] contains some twenty to thirty leagues, is very fine, and situated in latitude 44° 30'. It is very extensively cleared up. They plant in it a great quantity of Indian corn, which grows there finely. They plant likewise squashes, and sunflowers, from the seed of which they make oil, with which they anoint the head. . . . There are many very good vines and plums, which are excellent, raspberries, strawberries, little wild apples, nuts, and a kind of fruit of the form and color of small lemons, with a similar taste, but having an interior which is very good and almost like that of figs. The plant which bears this fruit is two and a half feet high, with but three or four leaves at most, which are of the shape of those of the fig tree, and each plant bears but two pieces of fruit. [*Podophyllum peltatum*, May apple?]

Among the Teton Dakota a remedy for pulmonary troubles was made by boiling sunflower heads from which the involucral bracts were first removed. The Teton had a saying that when the sunflowers were tall and in full bloom the buffaloes were fat and the meat good. A Pawnee said that the seeds pounded up with certain roots, the identity of which is not yet ascertained, were taken in the dry form, without further preparation, by women who became pregnant while still suckling a child. This was done in order that the suckling child should not become sick. The sunflower is mentioned in the Onondaga creation myth. [3]

---

[1] Charlevoix, Journal of a Voyage to North America, vol. I, p. 250.
[2] Champlain's Voyages, vol. III, p. 119.
[3] Hewitt, Iroquoian Cosmology, p. 174.

HELIANTHUS TUBEROSUS L. Jerusalem Artichoke. (Pl. 30, *b*.)
  Paⁿgi (Dakota).
  Paⁿk̃e (Omaha-Ponca).
  Paⁿk̃i (Winnebago).
  Kisu-sit (Pawnee) ; *kisu*, tapering; *sit*, long.
  The people of all the Nebraska tribes say they never cultivated
this plant, though they used its tubers for food. The Pawnee say
they ate them only raw, but the others, according to their own state-
ment, ate them either raw or boiled or roasted.
  Champlain reports seeing *Helianthus tuberosus* under cultivation
by Indians near Cape Cod in 1605 and again at Gloucester in 1606.[1]

RATIBIDA COLUMNARIS (Sims) D. Don.
  Wak̃cha-zi chik̃ala (Dakota), little *wak̃cha-zi* (*chikala*, little).
  An Oglala said the leaves and cylindrical heads of this plant were
used to make a beverage like tea.

ECHINACEA ANGUSTIFOLIA DC. Narrow-leaved Purple Cone Flower,
    Comb Plant. (Pl. 30, *a*.)
  Ichak̃pe-hu (Dakota), " whip plant " (*ichak̃pe*, whip).
  Mika-hi (Omaha-Ponca), " comb plant " (*mika*, comb) ; also called
    ikigahai, to comb; also called *iⁿshtogak̃te-hi*, referring to its use
    for an eye-wash (*iⁿshta*, eye).
  Ksapitahako (Pawnee), from *iksa*, hand; *pitahako*, to whirl. The
    name refers to its use by children in play when they take two
    stalks of it and whirl one round the other, the two stalks touch-
    ing by the two heads. Also called *Saparidu kahts*, mushroom
    medicine, so called from the form of the head, compared to a
    mushroom (*saparidu*).
  This plant was universally used as an antidote for snake bite and
other venomous bites and stings and poisonous conditions. *Echinacea* seems to have been used as a remedy for more ailments than
any other plant. It was employed in the smoke treatment for headache in persons and distemper in horses. It was used also as a
remedy for toothache, a piece being kept on the painful tooth until
there was relief, and for enlarged glands, as in mumps. It was
said that jugglers bathed their hands and arms in the juice of this
plant so that they could take out a piece of meat from a boiling kettle
with the bare hand without suffering pain, to the wonderment of
onlookers. A Winnebago said he had often used the plant to make
his mouth insensible to heat, so that for show he could take a live
coal into his mouth. Burns were bathed with the juice to give relief
from the pain, and the plant was used in the steam bath to render
the great heat endurable.

---

[1] Champlain's Voyages, pp. 82, 112.

SILPHIUM PERFOLIATUM L. Cup-plant, Square-stem, Angle-stem.

Zha tanga (Omaha-Ponca), big-weed, because of its size; ashude-kithe because of the use of root stocks in the smoke treatment; and zha-baho-hi, weed with angled stem (zha, weed; baho, having corners; hi, plant body).

Rake-ni-ozhu (Winnebago), weed that holds water (rake, weed; ni, water; ozhu, in, full or containing). Another name is rake-paraparatsh, square-weed (paraparatsh, square).

The root stock of this plant was very commonly used in the smoke treatment for cold in the head, neuralgia, and rheumatism. It was used also in the vapor bath. A Winnebago medicine-man said a decoction was made from the root stock which was used as an emetic in preparatory cleansing and lustration before going on the buffalo hunt or on any other important undertaking. It was thus used also for cleansing from ceremonial defilement incident to accidental proximity to a woman during her menstrual period.

SILPHIUM LACINIATUM L. Pilot Weed, Compass Plant, Gum Weed, Rosin Weed.

Chanshinshinla (Dakota), Teton dialect, chanshilshilya.

Zha-pa (Omaha-Ponca), bitter weed (zha, weed; pa, bitter), and makan-tanga, big medicine, or root.

Shokonwa-hu (Winnebago), gum plant (shokonwa, gum).

Kahts-tawas (Pawnee), rough medicine (kahtsu, medicine; tawas, rough); also called nakisokiit or nakisu-kiitsu (nakisu, pine; kiitsu, water).

The children gathered chewing gum from the upper parts of the stem, where the gum exudes, forming large lumps. The Omaha and Ponca say that where this plant abounds lightning is very prevalent, so they will never make camp in such a place. The dried root was burned during electrical storms that its smoke might act as a charm to avert lightning stroke. According to a Pawnee a decoction made from the pounded root was taken for general debility. This preparation was given to horses as a tonic by the Omaha and Ponca, and a Santee Dakota said his people used it as a vermifuge for horses.

AMBROSIA ELATIOR L. Ragweed.

White Horse, an Omaha medicine-man, said that this plant was an Oto remedy for nausea. In the treatment the surface of the abdomen of the patient was first scarified and a dressing of the bruised leaves was laid thereon.

BOEBERA PAPPOSA (Vent.) Rydb. Fetid Marigold, Prairie-dog Food.

Pizpiza-ta-wote (Dakota), prairie-dog food (pizpiza, prairie dog; wote, food; ta, genitive sign).

Pezhe piazhi (Omaha-Ponca), vile weed, referring to its odor (pezhe, herb; piazhi, bad, mean, vile).

Askutstat (Pawnee).

a. ECHINACEA ANGUSTIFOLIA INTERSPERSED WITH STIPA SPARTEA

Photo by courtesy of Department of Botany, Iowa State Agricultural College

b. TOPS AND TUBERS OF HELIANTHUS TUBEROSUS

LACINARIA SCARIOSA

The Teton Dakota say that this plant is always found in prairie-dog towns, and that these animals eat it. A decoction of *Boebera* together with *Gutierrezia* is used as a medicine for coughs in horses.

According to the Omaha it will cause nosebleed and they use it for that purpose to relieve headache. The leaves and tops, pulverized, were snuffed up the nostrils.

GUTIERREZIA SAROTHRAE (Pursh) Britton & Rusby. Broom-weed.

A decoction of the herb was given to horses as a remedy for too lax a condition of the bowels. They were induced to drink the bitter preparation by preventing them access to any other drink.

GRINDELIA SQUARROSA (Pursh) Dunal. Sticky Head.

Pte-ichi-yuku (Dakota), curly buffalo (*pte*, buffalo; *ichi*, together; *yuka*, curly, frizzly).

Pezhe-wasek (Omaha-Ponca), strong herb (*wasek*, strong).

Bakskitits (Pawnee), stick-head (*bak*, head; *skitits*, sticky).

Among the Teton Dakota a decoction of the plant was given to children as a remedy for colic. A Ponca said this was given also for consumption. The tops and leaves were boiled, according to a Pawnee informant, to make a wash for saddle galls and sores on horses' backs.

SOLIDAGO SP. Goldenrod.

Zha-sage-zi (Omaha-Ponca), hard yellow-weed (*zha*, weed; *sage*, hard; *zi*, yellow).

Goldenrod served the Omaha as a mark or sign in their floral calendar. They said that its time of blooming was synchronous with the ripening of the corn; so when they were on the summer buffalo hunt on the Platte River or the Republican River, far from their homes and fields, the sight of the goldenrod as it began to bloom caused them to say, "Now our corn is beginning to ripen at home."

ASTER SP. Prairie Aster.

An unidentified prairie aster was declared by a Pawnee to be the best material for moxa. The stems were reduced to charcoal which, in pieces a few millimeters in length, was set on the skin over the affected part and fired.

LACINIARIA SCARIOSA (L.) Hill. Blazing Star. (Pl. 30 A.)

Ao^ntashe (Omaha-Ponca); also called *maka^n-sagi*, hard medicine.

Kahtsu-dawidu or *kahtsu-rawidu* (Pawnee), round medicine (*kahtsu*, medicine; *rawidu* or *dawidu*, round).

A Pawnee said the leaves and corm were boiled together and the decoction was given to children for diarrhea. An Omaha made the statement that the corm after being chewed was blown into the nostrils of horses to enable them to run well without getting out of breath. It was supposed to strengthen and help them. The flower heads mixed with shelled corn were fed to horses to make them swift and put them in good condition.

ACHILLEA MILLEFOLIUM L. Yarrow, Milfoil.

Haⁿk-sintsh (Winnebago), woodchuck tail (*haⁿk*, woodchuck; *sintsh*, tail). Named from the appearance of the leaf.

An infusion of this herb was used by the Winnebago to bathe swellings. For earache a wad of the leaves, also the infusion, was put into the ear.

ARTEMISIA DRACUNCULOIDES Pursh. Fuzzy-weed.

Thasata-hi (Omaha-Ponca).

Rake-hiⁿshek (Winnebago), bushy weed, or fuzzy weed (*rake*, weed; *hiⁿshek*, bushy, fuzzy).

Kihapiliwus (Pawnee), broom (*kiharu*, broom; *piliwus*, to sweep).

Among the Winnebago the chewed root was put on the clothes as a love charm and hunting charm. The effect was supposed to be secured by getting to windward of the object of desire, allowing the wind to waft the odor of the herb thither. The Omaha ascribed the same powers to this species and used it in the same ways as they did the gray species of this genus next mentioned. It was used also in the smoke treatment. A Winnebago medicine-man said a handful of the tops of this species dipped into warm water served as a sprinkler for the body to relieve fevers. According to a Pawnee informant a decoction made of the tops was used for bathing as a remedy for rheumatism. Brooms for sweeping the lodge floor were made by binding together firmly a bundle of the tops. From this use comes its Pawnee name. The plant was liked for this purpose because of its agreeable, wholesome odor.

ARTEMISIA FRIGIDA Willd. Little Wild Sage.

Wia-ta-pezhihuta (Dakota), woman's medicine (*wia*, woman; *ta*, genitive sign; *pezhihuta*, medicine). The name refers to its use as explained farther on.

Pezhe-ḳota zhinga (Omaha-Ponca), little gray herb (*pezhi*, herb; *ḳota*, gray; *zhinga*, little).

Kiwoḳki (Pawnee).

A decoction of this species was used for bathing and was also taken internally by women when menstruation was irregular; hence the Dakota name.

ARTEMISIA GNAPHALODES Nutt. Wild Sage.

Pezhiḳota blaska (Dakota), flat *pezhihota*.

Pezhe-ḳota (Omaha-Ponca), gray herb.

Haⁿwiⁿska (Winnebago), white herb (*haⁿwiⁿ*, herb; *ska*, white).
Kiwaut (Pawnee).

All that is said of this species applies in general to all species of
Artemisia.

A bunch of *Artemisia* was sometimes used for a towel in old times.
A decoction of the plant was taken for stomach troubles and many
other kinds of ailments. It was used also for bathing. A person who
had unwittingly broken some taboo or had, touched any sacred
object must bathe with *Artemisia.* The immaterial essence or, to
use the Dakọta word, the *toⁿ*, of *Artemisia* was believed to be effectual as a protection against maleficent powers; therefore it was
always proper to begin any ceremonial by using *Artemisia* in order
to drive away any evil influences. As an example of the use among
the Omaha of *Artemisia* to avert calamity it is related that two
horses ran wild in the camp, knocking down the Sacred Tent. Two
old men, having caught the horses, rubbed them all over with wild
sage, and said to the young son of their owner, " If you let them do
that again, the buffaloes shall gore them."[1]

In the ceremonies of the installation of a chief among the Omaha
wild sage was used as a bed for the sacred pipes.[2] One of the personal names of men in the *Te-sinde* gens of the Omaha tribe is
Pezhe-hota.[3]

It has already been mentioned that the various species of *Artemisia* were used in old times as incense for the purpose of exorcising
evil powers. It has also been stated that cedar twigs or sweet grass,
either one, were used as incense to attract good powers. Some
Christian Indians also still employ all these species as incense for
these specific purposes, in church services, especially at Christmas,
Easter, Pentecost, and on occasion of funerals. The writer has
seen the use of *Artemisia* as an incense before a church door just
before the body was carried into the church. A small fire was made
before the steps of the church, *Artemisia* tops being used to raise a
cloud of smoke.

ARCTIUM MINUS Schk. Burdock.

This plant is a European introduction, probably not earlier than
the time of the first overland traffic by horses, mules, and oxen. It
is even now found commonly only along or near the old military
roads. It has been adopted by the Indians for medicinal use.
White Horse, of the Omaha, gave information, which he had obtained
from the Oto, of a decoction of the root being used as a remedy
for pleurisy.

---

[1] Dorsey, Omaha Sociology, p. 235.
[2] Ibid., p. 359.
[3] Ibid., p. 244.

LYGODESMIA JUNCEA (Pursh) D. Don. Skeleton Weed.

The Omaha and Ponca made an infusion of the stems of *Lygodesmia* for sore eyes. Mothers having a scanty supply of milk also drank this infusion in order to increase the flow.

In the north where *Silphium laciniatum* is not found *Lygodesmia* was used for producing chewing gum. The stems were gathered and cut into pieces to cause the juice to exude. When this hardened it was collected and used for chewing.

ANCIENT AND MODERN PHYTOCULTURE BY THE TRIBES

In former times the plants cultivated by the tribes inhabiting the region which has become the State of Nebraska comprised maize, beans, squashes, pumpkins, gourds, watermelons, and tobacco. I have not found evidence of more than one variety each of tobacco and watermelons. By disturbance of their industries and institutions incident to the European incursion they have lost the seed of the larger number of the crop plants they formerly grew. By search among several tribes I have been able to collect seed of many more varieties than any one tribe could furnish at the present time of the crops once grown by all these tribes. Of maize (*Zea mays*) they cultivated all the general types, dent corn, flint corn, flour corn, sweet corn, and pop corn, each of these in several varieties. Of beans (*Phaseolus vulgaris*) they had 15 or more varieties, and at least 8 varieties of pumpkins and squashes (*Pepo* sp.).

After diligent inquiry, the only cultivated crop plants of which I am able to get evidence are corn, beans, squashes and pumpkins, tobacco, and sunflowers. These are all of native origin in the Southwest, having come from Mexico by way of Texas. But a large number of plants growing wild, either indigenous or introduced by human agency, designedly or undesignedly, were utilized for many purposes. No evidence appears that any attempt was ever made looking to the domestication of any of these plants. The reason for this is that the necessary incentive was lacking, in that the natural product of each useful native plant was always available. In their semiannual hunting trips to the outlying parts of their domains, the Indians could gather the products belonging to each phytogeographic province. The crop plants which they cultivated, however, were exotics, and hence supplemented their natural resources, thereby forcing a distinct adjunct to the supply of provision for their needs.

But since the advent of Europeans the incentive is present to domesticate certain native plants which were found useful. This incentive arises from the fact that the influx of population has greatly reduced or almost exterminated certain species, and, even if the natural supply should suffice, the present restriction in range and movements of the Indians would prevent them from obtaining adequate quantities. This restriction results from the changed conditions of life and occupation, which necessitate their remaining at home attending to the staple agricultural crops or working at whatever other regular employment they have chosen. As a consequence, I have found in every tribe the incipient stage of domestication of certain wild fruits, roots, and other plant products for food or medicinal use, for smoking, or perfume. I have thus been privileged to see the beginnings of culture of certain plants which in future time may yield staple crops. In this way a lively conception can be formed of the factors which in prehistoric time brought about the domestication in Europe and Asia of our present well-known cultivated plants.

CONCLUSION

From this partial survey of the botanical lore of the tribes of the region under consideration we may fairly infer, from the general popular knowledge of the indigenous plants, that the tribes found here at the European advent had been settled here already for many generations and that they had given close attention to the floral life of the region. From the number of species from the mountain region, on one hand, and the woodland region, on the other, and also from the distant southwestern desert region, which they imported for various uses, we know they must have traveled extensively.

The several cultivated crops grown by the tribes of Nebraska are all of southwestern origin, probably all indigenous to Mexico. From this fact we can see that there was widely extended borrowing of culture from tribe to tribe.

The present study suggests the human agency as the efficient factor in the migration of some species of wild plants, or plants growing without cultivation. If this be the true explanation it affords the key to the heretofore puzzling isolation of areas occupied by certain species.

From the floral nomenclature of each tribe we find that they had at least the meager beginning of taxonomy. The names applied to plants show in many instances a faint sense of relationship of species to species.

My informants generally showed keen powers of perception of the structure, habits, and local distribution of plants throughout a wide range of observation, thus manifesting the incipiency of phytogeography, plant ecology, and morphology. The large number of species used and their many uses show considerable development of practical plant economy, or economic botany.

All these considerations of the relations between the aboriginal human population and the flora of the region are instructive to us as indicative of what must have been the early stages in the development of our own present highly differentiated botanical science. In this study of ethnic botany we have opportunity to observe the beginnings of a system of natural science which never came to maturity, being cut off in its infancy by the superposition of a more advanced stage of culture by an alien race upon the people who had attained the degree of culture we have here seen.

The following drawings by Bellamy Parks Jansen, prepared for this enlarged edition, illustrates selected plants described by Gilmore. The measurements provided are those of the plant specimens used for the drawings. Plants in the field may vary considerably in size.

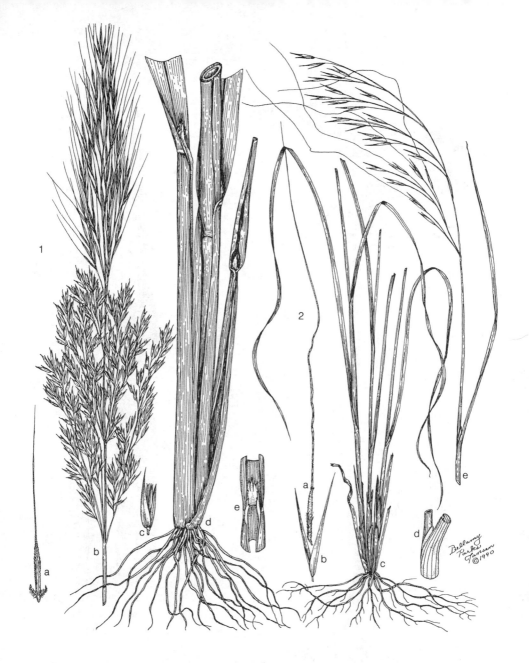

1. *Zizania aquatica*, wild rice. (a) Pistillate spikelet with awn. Height: 6.0 cm (2.4 in). (b) Inflorescence (flowering stalk). Height: 41.4 cm (16.5 in). (c) Staminate spikelet. Height: 1.3 cm (0.5 in). (d) Base with roots. Height of base: 35.8 cm (14.3 in). (e) Collar with ligule. Length: 2.8 cm (1.1 in). See page 15 and plate 3.

2. *Stipa spartea*, porcupine grass. (a) Awned lemma enclosing palea and caryopsis. Length: 18.7 cm (7.5 in). (b) Glume. Length: 3.1 cm (1.2 in). (c) Base with roots. Height: 27.9 cm (11.2 in). (d) Collar with ligule. Length: 1.2 cm (0.5 in). (e) Inflorescence. Height: 25.8 cm (10.3 in). See pages 14–15 and plate 2.

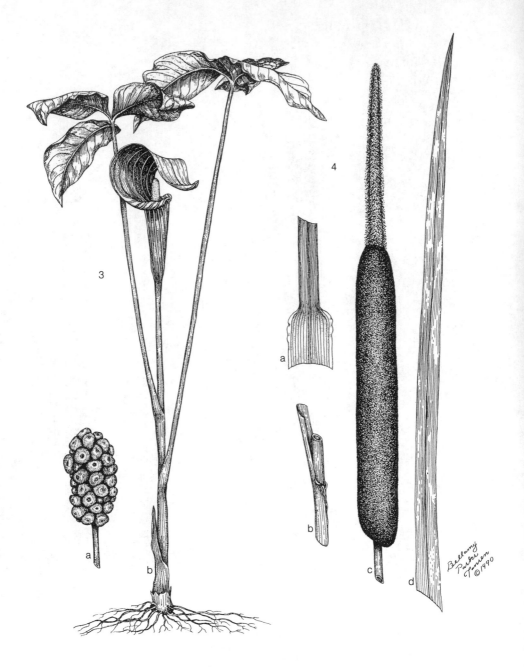

3. *Arisaema triphyllum*, jack-in-the-pulpit. (a) Fruit cluster (shiny red at maturity). Length: 7.1 cm (2.8 in). (b) Whole plant in bloom. Height: 29 cm (11.4 in). See page 17 and plate 4.

4. *Typha latifolia*, cattail. (a) Collar (open), no ligule present. Length shown: 7.5 cm (2.9 in). (b) Collar (closed) around stem. Length: 7.1 cm (2.8 in). (c) Infloresence. Length: 26 cm (10.22 in). (d) Leaf tip. Length: 30 cm (11.4 in). See pages 12–13 and plate 1b.

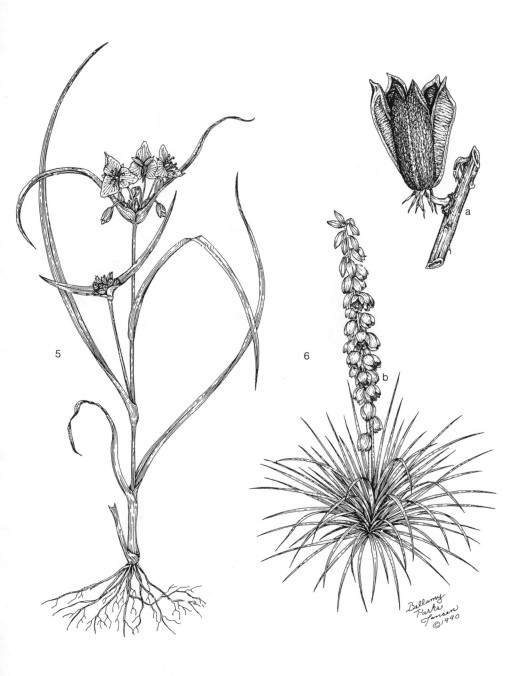

5. *Tradescantia occidentalis (T. virginica)*, spiderwort. Flowring plant. Length: 29.7 cm (11.7 in). See page 18 and plate 5a.

6. *Yucca glauca*, soapweed. (a) Open seed pod on stem. Length of seed pod: 5.1 cm (2 in). (b) Flowering plant. Size range: 2–5 feet. See page 19 and plates 7 and 8.

7

7. *Erythronium mesochoreum*, spring lily, snake lily. Flowering plants. Height: 14.5 to 16 cm (5.7 to 6.3 in). See page 19 and plate 6.

8. *Nelumbo lutea*, yellow lotus. (a) Fruit containing seeds. Size: 7.2 cm (2.8 in). (b) Leaf. Width across: 28.4 cm (11.2 in). (c) Flower. Width across: 15.5 cm (6.1 in). (d) Rhizome (root). Length: 13.5 cm (5.3 in). See page 27 and plate 10.

9. *Iris virginica var. shrevei (I. versicolor)*, blue flag. (a) Maturing fruit. Length: 6.8 cm (2.7 in). (b) Flower. Height: 7.5 cm (3 in). (c) Leaves. Length: 2 to 3 feet. (d) Base (rhizome). Size: 5.5 cm (2.2 in). See page 20 and plate 9.

10. *Aquilegia canadensis,* wild columbine. (a) Fruit. Length: 4.7 cm (1.9 in) (b) Flowering branch. Height: 25.4 cm (10 in). (c) Seed. Length: 1.5 mm (0.06 in). See pages 30–31 and plate 116.

11. *Thalictrum dasycarpum,* meadow rue. (a) Fruiting branch. Height: 6.9 cm (2.7 in). (b) Fruit. Size: 5 mm (0.02 in). (c) Flowering branch. Length: 23.1 cm (9.2 in). (d) Seed. Size: 2.5 mm (0.1 in). (e) Flower. Size: 1.3 cm (0.5 in). See page 28 and plate 11a.

12. *Sanguinaria canadensis*, bloodroot. (a) Seed. Size: 2 mm (0.08 in). (b) Fruit. Length: 4.7 cm (1.9 in). (c) Flowering plants. Height of larger plant: 21.2 cm (8.5 in). See page 31 and plate 12.

13. *Sagittaria latifolia*, arrowleaf. (a) Inflorescence. Length: 19 cm (7.5 in). (b) Base with roots. Height of plant: 26 cm (10.2 in). (c) Rhizome. Width: 0.38 cm (0.15 in). See page 13 and plate 1A.

14. *Prunus pumila* var. *besseyi* (*P. besseyi*), sand cherry. (a) Flower. Size: 0.4 cm (0.2 in). (b) Flowering branch. Height: 19.8 cm (7.8 in). (c) Fruiting branch. Diameter of fruit: 1.9 cm (0.75 in). See page 36 and plate 14.

15. *Cornus amomum*, red dogwood. (a) Flower. Size: 0.6 cm (0.2 in). (b) Fruiting branch. Length: 32.8 cm (12.9 in). (c) Fruit. Diameter: 0.7 cm (0.3 in). See pages 55–56 and plate 22.

16. *Psoralea esculenta*, tipsin, prairie turnip. (a) Flowering branch. Height: 15.4 cm (6.1 in). (b) Flower. Size: 1.5 cm (0.6 in). (c) Seed. Size: 0.5 cm (0.2 in). (d) Fruit. Size: 1.9 cm (0.75 in). (e) Root, showing turnip. Length of root section: 8.2 cm (3.2 in). See pages 40–41 and plates 15 and 16.

17. *Fragaria vesca* var. *americana (F. americana)*, wild strawberry. (a) Whole plant in bloom. Height (including root): 23 cm (9 in). (b) Stolon. Length: 5.6 cm (2.2 in). (c) Fruit. Length of larger fruit: 2.1 cm (0.8 in). See page 32 and plate 13a.

18. *Amphicarpaea bracteata (Falcata comosa)*, ground bean. (a) Flowering branch. Height: 28.4 cm (11.4 in). (b) Fruit before dehiscence (splitting). Length: 3.3 cm (1.3 in). (c) Fruit after dehiscence. Size: 3 cm (1.2 in). (d) Seed. Size: 0.4 cm (0.2 in). See pages 43–44 and plate 18.

19. *Apios americana (Glycine apios)*, Indian potato. (a) Flowering branch. Height: 29.7 cm (11.9 in). (b) Fruit. Length: 8.2 cm (3.3 in). (c) Flower. Size: 1 cm (0.4 in). (d) Tuber. Size: 5 cm (2 in). See pages 42–43 and plate 17.

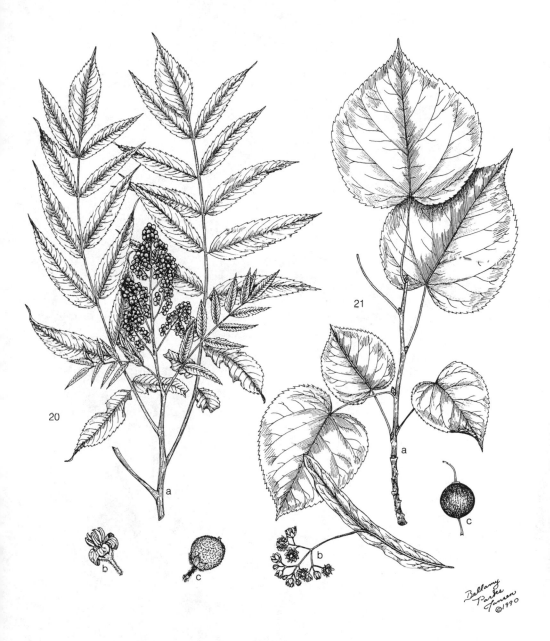

20. *Rhus glabra*, smooth sumac. (a) Fruiting branch (berries bright red at maturity). Height: 50 cm (20 in). (b) Flower. Size: 0.3 cm (0.1 in). (c) Fruit. Diameter: 0.45 cm (0.2 in). See pages 47–48 and plate 19a.

21. *Tilia americana*, basswood. (a) Branch with leaves. Length: 37 cm (15 in). (b) Flowers. Size of a flower: 1.5 cm (0.6 in). (c) Fruit. Diameter: 0.7 cm (0.3 in). See page 50 and plate 19b.

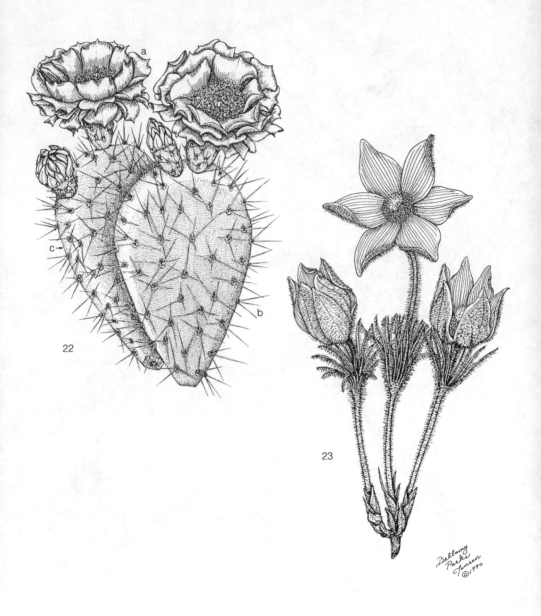

22. *Opuntia polyacantha (O. humifusa)*, prickly pear. (a) Flowers. Diameter: 7.8 cm (3.1 in). (b) Leaves (spines, needles). Length: 1.0 to 4.5 cm (0.4 to 1.8 in). (c) Stem. Length of stem on the left: 12 cm (4.8 in). See page 52 and plate 20a.

23. *Anemone patens (Pulsatilla patens)*, pasque flower. (a) Flowering branch. Height: 20.3 cm (8.1 in). See pages 28–30 and plate 1a.

24. *Sphondylium* L. subsp. *montanum* (Schleich.) Brig. (*Heracleum lanatum*), cow parsnip. (a) Flowering branch. Length: 16.5 cm (6.6 in). (b) Flower. Size: 1.5 mm (0.06 in). (c) Fruit. Size: 1.3 cm (0.5 in). (d) Leaf. Size: 26 cm (10.2 in). (e) Secondary umbel showing developing fruits. Size: 4 cm (1.6 in). See page 55 and plate 21.

25. *Shepherdia argentea (Lepargyrea argentea)*, buffalo berry. (a) Branch with leaves. Height: 21.2 cm (8.5 in). (b) Fruit (berry). Size: 9 mm (0.35 in). (c) Leaf, adaxial view (upper). Length: 3.3 cm (1.3 in). (d) Leaf, adaxial view (lower). Note: Leaf size varies greatly. See page 54 and plate 20b.

26. *Ipomoea leptophylla*, bush morning glory. (a) Flowering branch. Length: 29 cm (11.3 in). See page 58 and plates 25 and 26.

27. *Cucurbita foetidissima (Pepo foetidissima)*, wild gourd. (a) Flowering branch. Size: 30.8 cm (12.3 in). (b) Tendrils. Length at bottom of stem: 6.2 cm (2.5 in). (c) Fruit (gourd). Diameter: 5.4 cm (2.2 in). See pages 64–65 and plate 27a.

28. *Echinacea angustifolia* var. *angustifolia*, narrow-leaved purple cone flower. (a) Flowering branch. Height: 41.3 cm (16.5 in). (b) Ray flower. Length: 2.4 cm (1 in). (c) Disk flower. Length: 0.5 cm (0.2 in). (d) Floral bract. Size: 0.7 cm (0.3 in). See page 79 and plate 30a.

29. *Asclepias syriaca*, common milkweed. (a) Flowering branch. Length: 39.8 cm (15.9 in). (b) Flower. Size: 1 cm (0.4 in). (c) Fruit beginning dehiscence (splitting). Size: 5.5 cm (2.2 in). (d) Seed. Size: 2.2 cm (0.9 in). See pages 57–58 and plates 23 and 24.

30. *Helianthus tuberosus*, Jerusalem artichoke. (a) Flowering branch. Height: 22.4 cm (8.9 in). (b) Lower-leaf pair (opposite). Size: 12.1 cm (4.8 in). (c) Base with roots. Width of base: 1 cm (0.4 in). (d) Tuber. Length: 8 cm (3.2 in). See page 79 and plate 30b.

31. *Liatris aspera (Lacinaria scariosa)*, rough blazing star. (a) Flowering branch. Length: 26.3 cm (10.37 in). (b) Flower. Size: 0.8 cm (0.3 in). (c) Leaf. Length: 5.1 cm (2 in). See pages 81–82 and plate 30A.

GLOSSARY OF PLANT NAMES MENTIONED IN THIS MONOGRAPH

ARRANGED ALPHABETICALLY UNDER SCIENTIFIC NAME

Scientific name.	Common English name.	Dakota name.	Omaha name.	Winnebago name.	Pawnee name.
Acer negundo	Box elder	Chanshushka (also Tashkadaⁿ).	Zhaba ta-zhoⁿ	Naḥosh	Osako.
Acer saccharinum	Soft maple	Tahado	Wenu-shabethe-hu	Wⁿssep-hu	
Acer saccharum	Hard maple	Chaⁿ-ha saⁿ		Naⁿsaⁿk	
Achillea millefolium	Yarrow			Haⁿk-sintsh	
Acorus calamus	Sweet flag; calamus	Sinkpe ta wote	Makaⁿ-ninida	Makaⁿ-kereñ	Kahtsha-itu.
Acuan illinoensis	Spider bean		Pezhe-gasatho		Atikatsatsiks (also Kitsitsaris).
Allionia nyctaginea	Wild four-o'clock	Pofpfñ	Makaⁿ-wasek		Kahtstakat.
Allium mutabile	Wild onion	Pshiⁿ	Naⁿzhoⁿka-Mantanaha	Shiⁿhop	Osidiwa (Osidiwa Tsahiks).
Ambrosia elatior	Ragweed		Zhoⁿ-ñota		
Amelanchier alnifolia	June berry; Saskatoon	Wipazuka	Tehuⁿto-hi	Haz-shutsh	
Amorpha canescens	Lead plant; shoestring				
Amorpha fruticosa	Water string				Kitsuhast.
Andropogon furcatus	Blue joint grass		Ḣade zhidë		
Anemone canadensis	Anemone; wind flower		Te-zhinga Makaⁿ		
Anemone cylindrica			Wathibaba Makaⁿ		
Aquilegia canadensis	Wild columbine		Inu-bthoⁿ-kithe-sabë-hi		Skali-katit.
Arctium minus	Burdock				
Arisaema triphyllum	Jack-in-the-pulpit		Mikasi-makaⁿ		Nikso korórik kahtsu nitawáu.
Artemisia dracunculoides	Fuzzy weed	Wiⁿyaⁿ ta Pezhihuta	Thasáta-hi	Rake-hirshuk	Kiha-piliwus.
Artemisia frigida	Little wild sage	Pezhi-ñota Blaska	Pezhe-ñota zhinga		Kiwoñki.
Artemisia gnaphalodes	Wild sage	Pezhi-ñota Taⁿka	Pezhe-ñota	Haⁿwiⁿ-ska	
Artemisia tridentata; Artemisia cana	Sagebrush				
Asclepias syriaca	Big milkweed		Wañtha	Mahintsh	

Glossary of plant names mentioned in this monograph—Continued

ARRANGED ALPHABETICALLY UNDER SCIENTIFIC NAME—Continued

Scientific name.	Common English name.	Dakota name.	Omaha name.	Winnebago name.	Pawnee name.
Asclepias tuberosa.	Butterfly weed.		Makaⁿ-saka(also Kiu-makaⁿ)		
Astragalus caroliniana.	Little rattle pod.		Gaⁿsatho.		
Baptisia bracteata.	Black rattle pod.		Tdika-shanda Nuga.		Pira-kari.
Betula papyrifera.	Paper birch.	Taⁿpa (Teton dialect Chaⁿ-ha saⁿ).			
Boebera papposa.	Prairie-dog fennel; fetid marigold.	Piⁿpiza ta wote.	Pezhe Piazhi.		Askutstat.
Callirrhoe involucrata.	Purple mallow.	Pezhuta naⁿtiazilia.			
Caulophyllum thalictroides.	Blue cohosh.		Zhu-nakada Tanga Makaⁿ.		
Ceanothus americanus.	Indian tee; redroot.		Tabe-hi.		
Celastrus scandens.	Bittersweet.	Zuzecha ta wote.			
Celtis occidentalis.	Hackberry.	Yamnumnugapi.	Gubé.	Waké-warutsh.	Kaapsit.
Chamaesyce serpyllifolia.			Naze-ni-pezhe.		Kitsarius.
Chenopodium album.	Lamb's quarters.	Waⁿpe toto.	Saka-thidé.		
Citrullus citrullus.	Watermelon.	Saka yutapi.	Ḣade-bthaska.		
Coggswellia daucifolia.	Love seed.		Ninigaḣe zhidé.	Ruḣi-shutsh.	Rapahat.
Cornus amomum.	Kinnikinnick.	Chaⁿshasha.	Maⁿsa-ḣti-hi.		
Cornus asperifolia.	Dogwood.		Ninigahi-hte.		Nakipistatu.
Cornus stolonifera.	Kinnikinnick.	Chaⁿshasha-hi-chake.			
Corylus americana.	Hazelnut.	Uma.	Uⁿzhinga.	Huksik.	
Crataegus sp.	Thorn apple.	Taspaⁿ.	Taspaⁿ.	Chosaⁿwa.	
Cucurbita lagenaria.	Gourd.	Wamnu.			
Cuscuta paradoxa.	Dodder; love vine.			Makaⁿ-chahiwicho.	Hakastah-Kata.
Dicrophyllum marginatum.	Snow-on-the-mountain.				Karipika Tsitsiks.
Dasystephana puberula.	Gentian.	Pezhihuta Zi.			
Echinacea angustifolia.	Comb plant; purple cone-flower.	Ichaḣpehu.	Mika-hi (also Iⁿshtogalite-hi)		Ksapitahako.
Equisetum sp.	Scouring rush.		Maⁿde-ithe-shnaha.		Pakarut.
Erythrina flabelliformis.			Makaⁿ-zhidé.		

Botanical name	English name	Dakota	Omaha-Ponca	Winnebago	Pawnee
Euonymus atropurpurea	Burning bush; wahoo bush		Wanaña-i-monthi^n	Hedte-thutsh	
Erythronium mesochoreum	Spring lily				
Falcata comosa	Ground bean	Maka ta omnicha	Hi^{n}bthiabë		Atikuraru
Fragaria virginiana	Wild strawberry	Wazhushtecha	Bashtë	Honi^{n}L-boije	Aparu-huradu
Fraxinus pennsylvanica	Ash	Pseñti^n	Tashnanga-hi	Haz-s^{n}chek	Kiditako
Galium triflorum	Ladies' bouquet		Watñ-pezhe	Rak	
Geoprumnon crassicarpum	Buffalo pea; ground plum	Pte ta wote	Tdika-shanda		
Glycine apios	Indian potato	Mdo (Teton bio.)	Nu	Tdo	Its
Glycyrhiza lepidota	Wild licorice	Wi^{n}awizi	Pezhe-wasek		Pithahatusakitstsuhast
Grindelia squarrosa	Sticky head	Pte ichi-yuha	Pezi		Bakskitits
Grossularia missouriensis	Gooseberry	Wichañdeshka			
Gutierrezia sarothrae					
Gymnocladus dioica	Kentucky coffee tree	Walhañna	Na^{n}tita		Tohuts
Helianthus annuus	Sunflower	Wañcha Zizi	Zha-zi		Kirik-tara-kata
Helianthus tuberosus	Tuberous sunflower	Pa^{n}gi	Pa^{n}ñe		Kisusit
Hedeoma hispida	Pennyroyal	Maka^n Chiaka			
Heracleum lanatum	Cow parsnip; beaver root	Tado	Zhaba-maka^n		
Hicoria ovata	Hickory	Cha^{n}su	No^{n}si	Pa^{n}ji	Sahpakskitsu
Humulus americana	Hop	Cha^n-iyuwe			
Impatiens pallida	Wild touch-me-not				
Ionoxalis violacea	Sheep sorrel		Maka-skithë		Skidadihorit
Ipomoea leptophylla	Bush morning-glory		Hade-sathë		Kahts'-tuwiriki
Iris versicolor	Blue flag		Maka-skithë		
Juglans nigra	Black walnut		Tdagë	Chak	Sahtaku
Juniperus virginiana	Red cedar		Maazi		Tawatsako
Laciniaria scariosa	Blazing star	Wahuwapa-kichi Wa^{n}cna; Wahu^{n}wapa-kichi Namdu	Ao^{n}tashë (also Maka-saga)		Kahtsu-dawidu
Lathyrus ornatus	Wild sweet pea		Hi^{n}bthi-si Tanga		
Lepargyrea argentea	Buffalo berry	Mashti^{n}cha-puta	Zho^{n}hoje-wazhidë	Haz-shutz	Laritsits
Lespedeza capitata	Rabbit foot		Te-hu^{n}to^n-hi Nuga		
Lilium umbellatum	Flame lily				
Lithospermum canescens	Puccoon		Bazu-hi		
Lobelia cardinalis	Red lobelia; cardinal flower				
Lophophora williamsii	Peyote		Maka^n		
Lycoperdon gemmatum	Puffball	Hokshi-chekpa			

Glossary of plant names mentioned in this monograph—Continued

ARRANGED ALPHABETICALLY UNDER SCIENTIFIC NAME—Continued

Scientific name.	Common English name.	Dakota name.	Omaha name.	Winnebago name.	Pawnee name.
Lygodesmia juncea	Skeleton weed	Maka Chashlishi^n			
Malus ioensis	Iowa crab apple		She		
Malvastrum coccineum	Red false mallow	Heyoka ta pezhuta			
Melia azederach	China berry		Maka^n-zhide Saba		
Melilotus alba	Sweet clover	Wachang a iyechech a; Walipe wachanga	Pezhe-zonsta-ga^n		
Menispermum canadense	Moonseed		I^{n}gthahe-hazi-i-ta	Wanaghi-haz	Hakakut.
Mentha canadensis	Wild mint	Chiaka	Pezhe Nubtho^n		Kahts'-kiwahaaru.
Micrampelis lobata	Wild cucumber	Wahnahna hecha	Wata^n-gtha		Tsusatu.
Monarda fistulosa	Horsemint	Heliaka ta pezhuta; Hehaka ta wote	Pezhe-pa		Tsostu.
Monarda fistulosa (fragrant variety)	Washtemna	Walipe-washtemna	Pezhe-pa Mi^{n}ga (also Izna-kithe-iga-hi.)		
Morchella esculenta	Morel				
Nelumbo lutea	Water chinquapin; American lotus	Tewape	Tethawe	Tsherape	Tukawiu.
Nicotiana quadrivalvis		Cha^{n}di (Teton Cha^{n}li)			
Nicotiana rustica		Toka hupepe			
Nuttallia nuda (syn. Mentzelia nuda)					
Opuntia humifusa	Prickly pear	U^{n}kchela			Pidahatus.
Padus nana; Padus melanocarpa	Western chokecherry	Cha^{n}pa	Na^{n}pa Zhinga		Nahaapi-nakaaruts.
Panax quinquefolium	Ginseng				
Parosela aurea		Pezhuta-pa			
Parthenocissus quinquefolia	Virginia creeper		I^{n}gtha-hazi-ta		
Pentstemon grandiflorus	Wild foxglove				
Pepo foetidissima	Wild gourd	Wagamu^n pezhuta	Niashiga-maka^n		
Pepo pepo; Pepo maxima	Pumpkin; squash	Wagamu^n or Wakmu^n	Wata^n		

Petalostemum purpureum; Petalostemum candidum.	Prairie clover	Wanahcha	Maka-skithe		Kiha-piliwus-hawastat.
Phaseolus vulgaris.	Bean	Ommicha	Hinbthige	Honink	Atit.
Physalis heterophylla.	Ground cherry	Tamniohpa	Penigatush		
Physalis lanceolata.			Makan-bashashonshon	Harpok-hischásu	
Phytolacca americana.	Pokeberry				
Pinus murrayana.	Pine	Wazi			
Plantago major.	Large plantain				
Polystictus versicolor.	Tree-ears	Chan-nanpa	Sinié-makan		
Populus sargentii.	Cottonwood	Waga-chan	Maa-zhon		Natakaaru.
Prunus americana.	Wild plum	Kanpe	Kande	Kantsh	Niwaharit.
Prunus besseyi.	Sand cherry	Aonyeyapi (also Hastanka)	Nanpa Tanga		Kus aparu karuts.
Psoralea esculenta.	Tipsin	Tipsinna or Tinpsinna (Teton Tinpsila).	Nugthe	Tnlokéwihi	Patsuroka.
Psoralea tenuiflora.		Tichanicha.			
Pulsatilla patens.	Twin flower; pasque flower.	Hokshi Chekpa.			
Quercus macrocarpa.	Scrub oak.	Uskiyecha.	Tashka.	Chashke.	Patki Natawawi.
Quercus rubra.	Red oak.	Uta.	Buude.		Nahata Pahat.
Ratibida columnaris.		Wanhcha-zi Chikala.			
Rhus glabra.	Smooth sumac.	Chan-zi.	Minbdi-hi.		Nuppikt.
Ribes americanum.	Wild black currant.	Chap' ta haza.	Pezi Nuga.	Haz-ni-hu.	
Rosa pratincola.	Prairie wild rose.	Unzhinzhintka.	Wazhidé.		Pahatu.
Rubus occidentalis.	Wild black raspberry.	Takan-hecha.	Agthámungi.		Aparu.
Rubus strigosus.	Wild red raspberry.	....do.			
Rumex crispus.	Sour dock.	Shiakipi.			
Rumex hymenosepalus.	Canaigre.				
Sagittaria latifolia.	Arrowleaf.	Pshitola.	Sin.	Sinporo.	Kahts' pira kari.
Salix sp.	Willow.	Wanhpe-popa.	Thihe.	Runi.	Kirit.
Sambucus canadensis.	Elderberry.	Chaputa.	Wagathashka.		Kitapato.
Sanguinaria canadensis.	Bloodroot.		Minigathe makan wail.		Skirariu.
Savastana odorata.	Sweet grass.	Wachanga.	Pezhe zonsta.	Peti-hishuji.	Kataru.
Scirpus validus.	Bulrush.	Psa.	Sa.	Manuska.	Sistat.
Silphium laciniatum.	Gum weed; compass plant.	Chanshishinda (Teton Chanshilshila).	Zhapa (also Makan Tanga).	Shokanwa-hu.	Kahts' tawas (also Nakisoklit).

Glossary of plant names mentioned in this monograph—Continued

ARRANGED ALPHABETICALLY UNDER SCIENTIFIC NAME—Continued

Scientific name.	Common English name.	Dakota name.	Omaha name.	Winnebago name.	Pawnee name.
Silphium perfoliatum	Square stem; angle stem; cup plant.		Zha Tanga	Raké-ni-ozhu (also Raké Paraparatsh).	
Smilax herbacea				Toshunuk ahushke	
Solidago sp	Goldenrod		Zha Saga Zi		
Spartina michauxiana	Slough grass		Sidu-hi		Pitsuts.
Stipa spartea	Porcupine grass; needle grass		Mika-hi		
Symphoricarpos symphoricarpos	Coralberry	Zuzecha ta wote sapsapa	Irshtógalite-hi		
Symphoricarpos occidentalis	Buck brush	...do	...do		Skadiks.
Thalictrum dasycarpum	Zest-of-the-woods	Wazimna	Nisude-hi		
Thermopsis rhombifolia	False lupine		Hinde-hi	Hinshke	
Tilia americana	Linden	Hinte-chan	Hthiwathe-hi		Nakitsku.
Toxicodendron toxicodendron	Poison oak		Zhon-zi-zhu		
Toxylon pomiferum	Osage orange	Wanchá toto; Hcha-mdu toto			
Tradescantia virginica	Spiderwort	Wihuta-hu	Wahábigaskonthe	Ksho-hin	Kirit tacharush (also Hawahawa).
Typha latifolia	Cat-tail				
Ulmus americana	White elm	Pe	Ezhon Ska		Taisako Taka.
Ulmus fulva	Red elm; slippery elm	Pe-tutútupa	Ezhon Zhidé (also Ezhon Gthigthide).	Wakidikidik	Taisako Pahat.
Ulmus thomasi	Rock elm	Pe-itázipa	Ezhon Zi		
Urtica gracilis	Nettle		Hanuga-hi (also Manazhiha-hi).		
Usnea barbata	Lichen	Chan-wiziye			
Ustilago maydis	Corn smut				
Uva-ursi uva-ursi	Bearberry	Cha-hóloga pezhuta			
Verbena hastata	Wild blue verbena		Pezhe Makan		Nakasis.
Viburnum lentago	Black haw; sheepberry	Mna	Nanshaman	Wuwu	Akiwassas.

Viburnum opulus..........	Pemtina; "high-bush cranberry."	Wiátecha........			
Vitis cinerea........	Wild grape........	Hasta⁰ha⁰ka........	Hazi-hi........	Hap-sintsh........	Kisuts.
Washingtonia longistylis......	Sweet cicely........	Cha⁰pezhúta........	Shanga Maka⁰........		Kahts' Taraha.
Xanthoxalis stricta........	Yellow wood sorrel......		Ħade Sathé........		Skidadihortt.
Yucca glauca........	Spanish bayonet........	Hupéstola........	Duwáduwa-hi........		Chikida Kahtsu.
Zanthoxylum americanum......	Prickly ash........		Zho⁰ Pahithatha........		Hakasits.
Zea mays........	Corn........	Wamnáheza (Teton Wagmeza).	Wahába........		Nikiis.
Zizania aquatica........	Wild rice........	Psi⁰........	Siwaninde........	S.⁰	

Glossary of plant names mentioned in this monograph—Continued

ARRANGED ALPHABETICALLY UNDER DAKOTA NAME

Dakota name.	Scientific name.	Dakota name.	Scientific name.
Ao^{n}yeyapi (also Hasta^{n}ka).	Prunus besseyi.	Pte-ichi-yuña	Grindelia squarrosa.
Cha^{n}di (Teton dialect Cha^{n}li).	Nicotiana quadrivalvis.	Pte ta wote	Geoprumnon crassicarpum.
Cha^{n}haloga Pezhuta	Verbena hastata.	Saka yutapi	Citrullus citrullus.
Cha^n-ha sa^n	Acer saccharum.	Shiakipi	Rumex crispus.
Cha^n-iyuwe	Humulus americana.	Si^{n}kpe ta wote	Acorus calamus.
Cha^n-na^{n}pa	Polystictus versicolor.	Tado	Heracleum lanatum.
Cha^{n}pa	Padus nana; Padus melanocarpa.	Tahado	Acer saccharinum.
		Taka^{n}hecha	Rubus occidentalis.
Cha^n Pezhuta	Washingtonia longistylis.	Tamanioñpa	Physalis heterophylla.
Cha^n-shasha hi^{n}chaka	Cornus stolonifera.	Ta^{n}pa (Teton Cha^n-ha sa^n).	Betula papyrifera.
Cha^n-shasha	Cornus amomum.		
Cha^{n}shi^{n}shi^{n}la (Teton dialect Cha^{n}shilshilya)-	Silphium laciniatum.	Tashkada^n (also Cha^{n}shushka).	Acer negundo.
		Taspa^n	Cratægus sp.
Cha^{n}shushka (also Tashkada^n).	Acer negundo.	Tewape	Nelumbo lutea.
		Tichanicha	Psoralea tenuiflora.
Cha^n wiziye	Usnea barbata.	Tipsi^n	Psoralea esculenta.
Chap' ta haza	Ribes americanum.	Toka hupepe	Nuttallia nuda.
Chaputa	Sambucus canadensis.	U^{n}kchela	Opuntia humifusa.
Cha^{n}su	Hicoria ovata.	Uma	Corylus americana.
Cha^{n}zi	Rhus glabra.	Uskuyecha	Quercus macrocarpa.
Chiaka	Mentha canadensis.	Uta	Quercus rubra.
Hasta^{n}ha^{n}ka	Vitis cinerea.	Wachanga	Savastana odorata.
Ha^{n}te (or Ha^{n}te sha)	Juniperus virginiana.	Wachanga iyechecha (also Wañpe wachanga).	Melilotus alba.
Hasta^{n}ka	Prunus besseyi.		
Ḣeñaka ta pezhuta	Monarda fistulosa.		
Heyoka ta pezhuta	Malvastrum coccineum.	Waga-cha^n	Populus sargentii.
Hi^{n}te-cha^n	Tilia americana.	Wañcha toto; Ñchamdu toto.	Tradescantia virginica.
Hma	Juglans nigra.		
Hupestola	Yucca glauca.	Wañcha-zi chikala	Ratibida columnaris.
Ichañpe-hu	Echinacea angustifolia.	Wañcha-zizi	Helianthus annuus.
Ka^{n}te	Prunus americana.	Wagamu^n pezhuta	Pepo foetidissima.
Maka Cha^{n}shi^{n}shi^n	Lygodesmia juncea.	Wañnañnahecha	Micrampelis lobata.
Maka chiaka	Hedeoma hispida.	Wañnañina	Gymnocladus dioica.
Maka ta omnicha	Falcata comosa.	Wañpe popa	Salix sp.
Mashti^{n}cha-pute	Lepargyrea argentea.	Wañpe toto	Chenopodium album.
Mdo (Teton blo)	Glycine apios.	Wañpe wachanga (also Wachanga iyechecha).	Melilotus alba.
Mna	Viburnum lentago.		
Omnicha	Phaseolus vulgaris.	Wañpe washtemna	Monarda fistulosa (fragrant variety).
O^{n}zhi^{n}zhi^{n}tka	Rosa pratincola.		
Pa^{n}gi	Helianthus tuberosus.	Wamnu	Pepo pepo; Pepo maxima.
P'e-cha^n	Ulmus americana.		
P'e-itazipa	Ulmus thomasi.	Wamnaheza (Teton Wagmeza).	Zea mays.
P'e-tututupa	Ulmus fulva.		
Pezhi-ñota-blaska	Artemisia gnaphalodes.	Wamnuha	Cucurbita lagenaria.
Pezhihuta Zi	Dasystephana puberula.	Wanañcha	Petalostemum purpureum; Petalostemum candidum.
Pezhuta na^{n}tiazilia	Callirrhoe involucrata.		
Pezhuta pa	Parosela aurea.		
Pizpiza ta wote	Boebera papposa.	Wazhushtecha	Fragaria virginiana.
Poñpië	Allionia nyctaginea.	Wazi	Pinus sp.
Psa	Scirpus validus.	Wazima	Thalictrum dasycarpum.
Pseñti^n	Fraxinus sp.	Wia ta pezhihuta	Artemisia frigida.
Pshi^n	Allium mutabile.	Wichañdeshka	Grossularia missouriensis.
Pshitola	Sagittaria latifolia.		
Psi^n	Zizania aquatica.	Wihuta-hu	Typha latifolia.

Glossary of plant names mentioned in this monograph—Continued

ARRANGED ALPHABETICALLY UNDER DAKOTA NAME—Continued

Dakota name.	Scientific name.	Dakota name.	Scientific name.
Winawizi..............	Glycyrrhiza lepidota.	Zuzecha ta wote sapsapa.	Symphoricarpos sym-
Wipázuka...............	Amelanchier alnifolia.		phoricarpos; Symphor-
Yamnumnugapi........	Celtis occidentalis.		icarpos occidentalis.
Zuzećha ta wote........	Celastrus scandens.		

ARRANGED ALPHABETICALLY UNDER OMAHA NAME

Omaha name.	Scientific name.	Omaha name.	Scientific name.
Agthámungi.............	Rubus occidentalis.	Makan-bashashónshon...	Physalis lanceolata.
Aóntashi (also Makán-sagi).	Laciniaria scariosa.	Makan-ninida...........	Acorus calamus.
Bashte...................	Fragaria virginiana.	Makan-sagi (also Aon-tashe).	Laciniaria scariosa.
Bazu-hi.................	Lithospermum canescens	Makan-saka (also Kiu-makan).	Asclepias tuberosa.
Buude..................	Quercus rubra.	Makan- skithe..........	Humulus americana.
Duwáduwa-hi..........	Yucca glauca.	Makan-skithe...........	Iris versicolor.
Ezhon..................	Ulmus sp.	Makan-skithe...........	Petalostemum purpur-
Ezhon-ska.............	Ulmus americana.		eum; Petalostemum
Ezhon-zi...............	Ulmus thomasi.		candidum.
Ezhon-zhidë (or Ezhon-gthigthidë).	Ulmus fulva.	Makan-tanga............	Siliphium laciniatum.
Gansatho..............	Astragalus caroliniana.	Makan-wasek...........	Allionia nyctaginea.
Gubë..................	Celtis occidentalis.	Makan-zhide...........	Erythrina flabelliformis.
Hazi..................	Vitis cinerea.	Makan-zhide sabe.......	Melia azedarach.
Hinbthiabë............	Falcata comosa.	Mansa-liti-hi...........	Cornus asperifolia.
Hinbthinge............	Phaseolus vulgaris.	Manzhonka mantanaha..	Allium mutabile.
Hinbthi-si-tanga........	Lathyrus ornatus.	Minbdi-hi..............	Rhus glabra.
Hinde-hi..............	Tilia americana.	Mika-hi (also Inshtogahi-te-hi).	Echinacea angustifolia.
Hthi-wathe-hi..........	Toxicodendron toxico-dendron.	Mika-hi.................	Stipa spartea.
Hanuga-hi (also Mana-zhiha-hi).	Urtica gracilis.	Mikasi makan	Arisaema triphyllum.
		Minigathe-makan-waü ..	Sanguinaria canadensis.
Hade-bthaska..........	Cogswellia daucifolia.	Nanpa Tanga...........	Prunus besseyi.
Hade-sathë............	Ionoxalis violacea; Xan-thoxalis stricta.	Nanpa Zhinga..........	Padus nana; Padus me-lanocarpa.
Hade-zhidë............	Andropogon furcatus.	Nanshaman..............	Viburnum lentago.
Ingtha hazi itai.........	Parthenocissus quinque-folia.	Nantita.................	Gymnocladus dioica.
		Naze-ni Pezhe..........	Chamaesyce serpyllifolia.
Ingtha hazi itai.........	Menispermum cana-dense.	Niashiga Makan.........	Pepo foetidissima.
		Ninigahe-liti............	Cornus stolonifera.
Inubthonkithe-sabë-hi...	Aquilegia canadensis.	Ninigahe Zhide.........	Cornus amomum.
Inshtogahte-hi..........	Symphoricarpos sym-phoricarpos; Sympho-ricarpos occidentalis.	Nisude-hi..............	Thalictrum dasycarpum.
		Nonsi.................	Hicoria ovata.
		Nu.....................	Glycine apios.
Izna-kithe-iga-hi (also Pezhe-pa minga.	Monarda fistulosa var.	Nugthe.................	Psoralea esculenta.
Kande.................	Prunus americana.	Panhe.................	Helianthus tuberosus.
Kiu-makan (also Makan-saka).	Asclepias tuberosa.	Pehe..................	Cucurbita lagenaria.
Maa-zhon..............	Populus sargentii.	Pezhi Bthasha	Cogswellia daucifolia.
		Pezhe hota.............	Artemisia gnaphalodes.
Maazi.................	Juniperus virginiana.	Pezhe-hote Zhinga......	Artemisia frigida.
Mande-idhe-shnaha......	Equisetum sp.	Pezhe Piazhi...........	Boebera papposa.
Makan.................	Lophophora willamsii.	Pezhe-gasatho..........	Acuan illinoensis.
		Pezhe-makan...........	Verbena hastata.

Glossary of plant names mentioned in this monograph—Continued

ARRANGED ALPHABETICALLY UNDER OMAHA NAME—Continued

Omaha name.	Scientific name.	Omaha name.	Scientific name.
Pezhe 'Nubthon	Mentha canadensis.	Thasata-hi	Artemisia dracunculoides.
Pezhe-pa	Monarda fistulosa.		
Pezhe-pa Minga	Monarda fistulosa (fragrant variety).	Thihe-sage-hi	Salix sp.
		Unzhinga	Corylus americana.
Pezhe Zonsta	Savastana odorata.	Wagathashka	Sambucus canadensis.
Pezhe-zonsta egan	Melilotus alba.	Wahaba	Zea mays.
Pezhe-wasek	Grindelia squarrosa.	Wahabigaskonthe	Typha latifolia.
Pe-igatush	Physalis heterophylla.	Wahaba-hthi	Ustilago maydis.
Pezi	Grossularia missouriensis.	Wahtha	Asclepias syriaca.
		Wananha-i-monthin	Euonymus atropurpurea.
Pezi nuga	Ribes americanum.	Watan	Pepo pepo; Pepo maxima.
Sa-hi	Scirpus validus.		
Saka-thide	Citrullus citrullus.	Watangtha	Micrampelis lobata.
Shanga makan	Washingtonia longistylis.	Wathíbaba makan	Anemone cylindrica.
		Waü pezhe	Galium triflorum.
She	Malus ioensis.	Wenu shabethe hi	Acer saccharinum.
Sinie makan	Plantago major.	Wazhide	Rosa pratincola.
Sin	Sagittaria latifolia.	Zhaba makan	Heracleum lanatum.
Sinwaninde	Zizania aquatica.	Zhaba ta zhon	Acer negundo.
Tabe-hi	Ceanothus americana.	Zha-pa (also Makantanga).	Silphium laciniatum.
Tashka	Quercus macrocarpa.		
Tashnanga-hi	Fraxinus sp.	Zha-sage-zi	Solidago sp.
Taspan	Crataegus sp.	Zha-tanga	Silphium perfoliatum.
Tdika-shanda	Geoprumnon crassicarpum.	Zha-zi	Helianthus annuus.
		Zhon-hoji-wazhide	Lepargyrea argentea.
Tdika-shanda Nuga	Baptisia bracteata.	Zhon-hoda	Amelanchier alnifolia.
Tdage	Juglans nigra.	Zhon-pahíthatha	Zanthoxylum americanum.
Te-hunton-hi	Amorpha canescens.		
Te-hunton-hi Nuga	Lespedeza capitata.	Zhon-zi-zhu	Toxylon pomiferum.
Tethawe	Nelumbo lutea.	Zhu - nakada - tanga - makan.	Caulophyllum thalictroides.
Te-zhinga Makan	Anemone canadensis.		

ARRANGED ALPHABETICALLY UNDER WINNEBAGO NAME

Winnebago name.	Scientific name.	Winnebago name.	Scientific name.
Chak	Juglans nigra.	Honink	Phaseolus vulgaris.
Chashke	Quercus macrocarpa.	Honink-boije	Falcata comosa.
Chosanwa	Crataegus sp.	Huksik	Corylus americana.
Hank-sintsh	Achillea millefolium.	Kantsh	Prunus americana.
Hanpok-hischasu	Physalis lanceolata.	Ksho-hin	Typha latifolia.
Hap-sintsh	Vitis cinerea.	Mahintsh	Asclepias syriaca.
Hanwin-ska	Artemisia gnaphalodes.	Makan-chahiwi-cho	Dasystephana puberula.
Haz-ni-hu	Rhus glabra.	Makan-kereli	Acorus calamus.
Haz-ponoponoh	Grossularia missouriensis.	Manuska	Savastana odorata.
		Mansi-hotsh	Cornus asperifolia.
Haz-shchek	Fragaria virginiana.	Nahosh	Acer negundo.
Haz-shutsh	Amelanchier alnifolia.	Nanpashakanak	Gymnocladus dioica.
Haz-shutsh	Lepargyrea argentea.	Nansank	Acer saccharum.
Hedte-shutsh	Erythronium mesochoreum.	Panja	Hicoria ovata.
		Panhi	Helianthus tuberosus.
Hinshke	Tilia americana.	Peli-hishuji	Sanguinaria canadensis.

Glossary of plant names mentioned in this monograph—Continued

ARRANGED ALPHABETICALLY UNDER WINNEBAGO NAME—Continued

Winnebago name.	Scientific name.	Winnebago name.	Scientific name.
Rak	Fraxinus sp.	Tdo	Glycine apios.
Rake-hiⁿshuk	Artemisia dracunculoides.	Tdokewihi	Psoralea esculenta.
		Toshunuk-ahunshke	Smilax herbacea.
Rakĕ-ni-ozhu (also Rakĕ-paraparatsh).	Silphium perfoliatum.	Tsherape	Nelumbo lutea.
		Wakĕ-warutsh	Celtis occidentalis.
Ruḣi	Salix sp.	Wakidikidik	Ulmus fulva.
Ruḣi-shutsh	Cornus amomum.	Wanaghi-haz	Menispermum canadense.
Shiⁿhop	Allium mutabile.		
Shokaⁿwa-hu	Silphium laciniatum.	Wissep-hu	Acer saccharinum.
Siⁿ	Zizania aquatica.	Wuwu	Viburnum lentago.
Siⁿporo	Sagittaria latifolia.		

ARRANGED ALPHABETICALLY UNDER PAWNEE NAME

Pawnee name.	Scientific name.	Pawnee name.	Scientific name.
Akiwasas	Viburnum lentago.	Kirit	Sagittaria latifolia.
Aparu	Rubus occidentalis.	Kirit-tacharush (also Hawahawa).	Typha latifolia.
Aparu-huradu	Fragaria virginiana.		
Askutstat	Boebera papposa.	Kisusit	Helianthus tuberosus.
Atit	Phaseolus vulgaris.	Kisuts	Vitis cinerea.
Atit-kuraru	Falcata comosa.	Kitapato	Salix sp.
Atikatsatsiks (also Kitsitsaris).	Acuan illinoensis.	Kitsitsaris (also Atikatsatsiks).	Acuan illinoensis.
Bakskitits	Grindelia squarrosa.	Kitsarius	Chenopodium album.
Chakida kahtsu	Yucca glauca.	Kitsuhast	Amorpha fruticosa.
Hakakut	Menispermum canadense.	Kiwoḣki	Artemisia frigida.
		Ksapitahako	Echinacea angustifolia.
Hakasits	Zanthoxylum americanum.	Kus aparu karuts	Prunus besseyi.
		Laritsits	Lepargyrea argentea.
Hakastah-kata	Cuscuta paradoxa.	Nahaapi nakaaruts	Padus nana; P. melanocarpa.
Hawahawa (also Kirit-tacharush).	Typha latifolia.		
		Nahata pahat	Quercus rubra.
Its	Glycine apios.	Nakasis	Uva-ursi uva-ursi.
Kaapsit	Celtis occidentalis.	Nakipistatu	Cornus stolonifera.
Kahts'-ha-itu	Acorus calamus.	Nakitsku	Toxylon pomiferum.
Kahts'-kiwaharu	Mentha canadensis.	Natakaaru	Populus sargentii.
Kahtsu dawidu	Laciniaria scariosa.	Nikakitspak	Physalis heterophylla.
Kahts' pira kari	Rumex hymenosepalus.	Nikiis	Zea mays.
Kahts' Takat	Allionia nyctaginea.	Nikso korórik kahtsu nitawäü.	Arisaema triphyllum.
Kahts'Taraha	Washingtonia longistylis.		
Kahts'-Tawas (also Nakisokiit).	Silphium laciniatum.	Niwaharit	Prunus americana.
		Nuppikt	Rhus glabra.
Kahts'-tuwiriki	Ipomoea leptophylla.	Osako	Acer negundo.
Karipika	Asclepias syriaca.	Osidiwa (or Osidiwa Tsahiks).	Allium mutabile.
Karipika tsitsiks	Dichrophyllum marginatum.		
		Pahatu	Rosa pratincola.
Kataaru	Savastana odorata.	Pakarut	Equisetum sp.
Kiditako	Fraxinus sp.	Parus-as	Lespedeza capitata.
Kiha-piliwus	Artemisia dracunculoides.	Patki natawawi	Quercus macrocarpa.
		Patsuroka	Psoralea esculenta.
Kiha-piliwus-hawastat	Petalostemum purpureum; P. candidum.	Pidahatus	Opuntia humifusa.
		Pira-kari	Baptisia bracteata.
Kirik-tara-kata	Helianthus annuus.	Pithahatusakits Tsuhast	Glycyrhiza lepidota.

Glossary of plant names mentioned in this monograph—Continued

ARRANGED ALPHABETICALLY UNDER PAWNEE NAME—Continued

Pawnee name.	Scientific name.	Pawnee name.	Scientific name.
Pitsuts	Stipa spartea.	Taitsako	Ulmus sp.
Rapahat	Cornus amomum.	Taitsako pahat	Ulmus fulva.
Sahpakskiisu	Hicoria ovata.	Taitsako taka	Ulmus americana.
Sahtaku	Juglans nigra.	Tawatsaako	Juniperus virginiana.
Sistat	Scirpus validus.	Tohuts	Gymnocladus dioica.
Skadiks	Thalictrum dasycarpum.	Tsostu	Monarda fistulosa (fragrant variety).
Skali-katit	Aquilegia canadensis.		
Skidadihorit	Ionoxalis violacea; Xanthoxalis stricta.	Tsusahtu	Monarda fistulosa.
Skirariu	Sambucus canadensis.	Tukawiu	Nelumbo lutea.

ARRANGED ALPHABETICALLY UNDER COMMON ENGLISH NAME

Common English name.	Scientific name.	Common English name.	Scientific name.
American elm	Ulmus americana.	Chokecherry	Padus nana; Padus melanocarpa.
American lotus	Nelumbo lutea.		
Anemone	Anemone canadensis.	Comb plant	Echinacea angustifolia.
Angle stem	Silphium perfoliatum.	Compass plant	Silphium laciniatum.
Ash	Fraxinus pennsylvanica.	Corn	Zea mays.
		Corn smut	Ustilago maydis.
Arrowleaf	Sagittaria latifolia.	Cottonwood	Populus sargentii.
Bean	Phaseolus vulgaris.	Cow parsnip	Heracleum lanatum.
Bearberry	Uva-ursi uva-ursi.	Cup plant	Silphium perfoliatum.
Beaver root	Heracleum lanatum.	Coralberry	Symphoricarpos symphoricarpos.
Big milkweed	Asclepias syriaca.		
Birch, paper	Betula papyrifera.	Dodder	Cuscuta paradoxa.
Bittersweet	Celastrus scandens.	Elderberry	Sambucus canadensis.
Black haw	Viburnum lentago.	Elm	Ulmus.
Black rattle pod	Baptisia bracteata.	False lupine	Thermopsis rhombifolia.
Black walnut	Juglans nigra.	Fetid marigold	Boebera papposa.
Blazing star	Laciniaria scariosa.	Flame lily	Lilium umbellatum.
Bloodroot	Sanguinaria canadensis.	Fragrant bedstraw	Galium triflorum.
Blue cohosh	Podophyllum peltatum.	Fuzzy weed	Artemisia dracunculoides.
Blue flag	Iris versicolor.		
Blue joint grass; blue stem grass.	Andropogon furcatus.	Gentian	Dasystephana puberula.
		Ginseng	Panax quinquefolium.
Box elder	Acer negundo.	Goldenrod	Solidago.
Buck brush	Symphoricarpos occidentalis.	Gooseberry	Grossularia missouriensis.
Buffalo pea	Geoprumnon crassicarpum.	Gourd	Cucurbita lagenaria.
		Ground bean	Falcata comosa.
Buffalo berry	Lepargyrea argentea.	Ground cherry	Physalis heterophylla.
Bulrush	Scirpus validus.	Ground plum	Geoprumnon crassicarpum.
Burdock	Arctium minus.		
Burning bush	Euonymus atropurpurea.	Gum weed	Silphium laciniatum.
		Hackberry	Celtis occidentalis.
Bush morning-glory	Ipomoea leptophylla.	Hard maple	Acer saccharum.
Butterfly weed	Asclepias tuberosa.	Hazelnut	Corylus americana.
Calamus	Acorus calamus.	Hickory	Hicoria ovata.
Canaigre	Rumex hymenosepalus.	Hop	Humulus americana.
Cardinal flower	Lobelia cardinalis.	Horsemint	Monarda fistulosa.
Cat-tail	Typha latifolia.	Indian potato	Glycine apios.
Cedar	Juniperus virginiana.	Indian tea	Ceanothus americana.
China berry	Melia azedarach.	Iowa crabapple	Malus ioensis.

Glossary of plant names mentioned in this monograph—Continued

ARRANGED ALPHABETICALLY UNDER COMMON ENGLISH NAME—Continued

Common English name.	Scientific name.	Common English name.	Scientific name.
Iris	Iris versicolor.	Sand cherry	Prunus besseyi.
Jack-in-the-pulpit	Arisaema triphyllum.	Saskatoon	Amelanchier alnifolia.
Juneberry	Amelanchier alnifolia.	Scouring rush	Equisetum.
"Jerusalem artichoke"	Helianthus tuberosus.	Scrub oak	Quercus macrocarpa.
Kentucky coffee tree	Gymnocladus dioica.	Sheepberry	Viburnum lentago.
Kinnikinnick	Cornus amomum; Cornus stolonifera.	Sheep sorrel	Ionoxalis violacea.
		Shoestring	Amorpha canescens.
Ladies' bouquet	Galium triflorum.	Skeleton weed	Lygodesmia juncea.
Lamb's-quarters	Chenopodium album.	Slippery elm	Ulmus fulva.
Lichen	Usnea barbata.	Slough grass	Spartina michauxiana.
Linden	Tilia americana.	Smooth sumac	Rhus glabra.
Little rattle pod	Astragalus caroliniana.	Snowberry	Symphoricarpos occidentalis.
Lobelia	Lobelia cardinalis.		
Love seed	Cogswellia daucifolia.	Snow-on-the-mountain	Dicrophyllum marginatum.
Love vine	Cuscuta paradoxa.		
Moonseed	Menispermum canadense.	Soft maple	Acer saccharinum.
		Sour dock	Rumex crispus.
Needle grass	Stipa spartea.	Spanish bayonet	Yucca glauca.
Nettle	Urtica gracilis.	Spider bean	Acuan illinoensis.
Osage orange	Toxylon pomiferum.	Spiderwort	Tradescantia virginica.
Paper birch	Betula papyrifera.	Spider lily	Tradescantia virginica.
Pasque flower	Pulsatilla patens.	Spring lily	Erythronium mesochoreum.
Pembina	Viburnum opulus.		
Pennyroyal	Hedeoma hispida.	Square stem	Silphium perfoliatum.
Peyote	Lophophora williamsii.	Squash	Pepo maxima.
Pine	Pinus murrayana.	Sticky head	Grindelia squarrosa.
Plantain	Plantago major.	Sunflower	Helianthus annuus.
Poison oak	Toxicodendron toxicodendron.	Sweet clover	Melilotus alba.
		Sweet cicely	Washingtonia longistylis.
Pokeberry	Phytolacca americana.		
Porcupine grass	Stipa spartea.	Sweet flag	Acorus calamus.
Prairie-dog fennel	Boebera papposa.	Sweet grass	Savastana odorata.
Prairie wild rose	Rosa pratincola.	Switch grass	Panicum virgatum.
Prairie clover	Petalostemum purpureum; Petalostemum candidum.	Thorn apple	Crataegus.
		Tipsin	Psoralea esculenta.
		Tobacco	Nicotiana quadrivalvis; Nicotiana rustica; Nicotiana tabacum.
Prickly ash	Zanthoxylum americanum.		
Prickly pear	Opuntia humifusa.	Tree ears	Polystictus versicolor.
Puccoon	Lithospermum canescens.	Tuberous sunflower	Helianthus tuberosus.
		Twin flower	Pulsatilla patens.
Puffball	Lycoperdon gemmatum.	Virginia creeper	Parthenocissus quinquefolia.
Pumpkin	Pepo pepo.		
Purple coneflower	Echinacea angustifolia.	Wahoo bush	Euonymus atropurpureus.
Purple mallow	Callirrhoe involucrata.		
Rabbit foot	Lespedeza capitata.	Washtemna	Monarda fistulosa (fragrant variety).
Ragweed	Ambrosia elatior.		
Red false mallow	Malvastrum coccineum.	Water chinquapin	Nelumbo lutea.
Red elm	Ulmus fulva.	Watermelon	Citrullus citrullus.
Red haw	Crataegus.	Water string	Amorpha fruticosa.
Red oak	Quercus rubra.	White elm	Ulmus americana.
Redroot	Ceanothus americana.	Wild black currant	Ribes americanum.
Rock elm	Ulmus thomasi.	Wild black raspberry	Rubus occidentalis.
Sagebrush	Artemisia cana; Artemisia tridentata.	Wild blue verbena	Verbena hastata.
		Wild columbine	Aquilegia canadensis.

Glossary of plant names mentioned in this monograph—Continued

ARRANGED ALPHABETICALLY UNDER COMMON ENGLISH NAME—Continued

Common English name.	Scientific name.	Common English name.	Scientific name.
Wild crab apple.........	Malus ioensis.	Wild rose, prairie.......	Rosa pratincola.
Wild cucumber.........	Micrampelis lobata.	Wild sage, big...........	Artemisia gnaphalodes.
Wild four-o'clock........	Allionia nyctaginea.	Wild sage, little.........	Artemisia frigida.
Wild foxglove...........	Pentstemon grandiflorus.	Wild strawberry........	Fragaria virginiana; Fragaria americana.
Wild gourd..............	Pepo foetidissima.		
Wild grape..............	Vitis cinerea.	Wild sweet pea..........	Lathyrus ornatus.
Wild licorice............	Glycyrhiza lepidota,	Wild touch-me-not......	Impatiens pallida.
Wild mint..............	Mentha canadensis.	Willow..................	Salix.
Wild onion.............	Allium mutabile.	Wind flower............	Anemone canadensis.
Wild red raspberry......	Rubus strigosus.	Yarrow.................	Achillea millefolium.
Wild plum..............	Prunus americana.	Yellow wood sorrel......	Xanthoxalis stricta.
Wild rice...............	Zizania aquatica.	Zest-of-the-woods........	Thalictrum dasycarpum.

BIBLIOGRAPHY

BARKLEY, T. M. et al., *eds.* Flora of the Great Plains. Lawrence: University Press of Kansas, 1986.

BEVERLY, ROBERT. The history and present state of Virginia, by a native and inhabitant. London, 1705.

BLAIR, EMMA, *tr. and ed.* The Indian tribes of the Upper Mississippi Valley and region of the Great Lakes as described by Nicolas Perrot, Bacqueville de la Potherie, Morrell Marston, and Thomas Forsyth. Vols. I–II. Cleveland, 1911–12.

BRADBURY, JOHN. Travels in the interior of America in the years 1809, 1810, and 1811. 2d ed. London, 1819.

CANDOLLE, ALPH. DE. Geographie botanique. Tome 2. Paris and Geneva, 1855.

CHAMPLAIN, SAMUEL DE. Voyages of Samuel de Champlain. Translated from the French by Charles Pomeroy Otis, with memoir by Edmund F. Slafter. 3 vols. Boston, 1878–1882. (*Prince Society Publications*, vols. xi, xii, and xiii.)

CHARLEVOIX, PIERRE DE. Journal of a voyage to North-America. Vols. I–II. London, 1761.

CHITTENDEN, HIRAM MARTIN, *and* RICHARDSON, ALFRED T. Life, letters, and travels of Father Pierre-Jean De Smet, S. J., 1801–1873. Vols. I–IV. New York, 1905.

CLEMENTS, FREDERIC E. *See* POUND, ROSCOE, *and* CLEMENTS.

CONZATTI, C. Los géneros vegetales Mexicanos. Mexico, 1903.

COULTER, JOHN M. Botany of Western Texas. *Cont. U. S. Nat. Herb.*, vol. II, Washington, 1891–94.

COX, ISAAC JOSLIN, *ed.* The journeys of Rene Robert Cavelier Sieur de La Salle. Vols. I–II. New York, 1905.

DENSMORE, FRANCES. Chippewa music. Part II. *Bull. 53, Bur. Amer. Ethn.*, Washington, 1913.

DE SMET, PIERRE-JEAN. *See* CHITTENDEN *and* RICHARDSON.

DORSEY, JAMES OWEN. Omaha sociology. In *Third Ann. Rept. Bur. Ethn.*, pp. 205–370, Washington, 1884.

———. The Ǵegiha language. *Cont. to N. Amer. Ethn.*, vol. VI, Washington, 1890.

———. A study of Siouan cults. In *Eleventh Ann. Rept. Bur. Ethn.*, pp. 361–544, Washington, 1894.

DU PRATZ. *See* LE PAGE DU PRATZ.

FEWKES, JESSE WALTER. Two summers' work in Pueblo ruins. In *Twenty-second Rept. Bur. Amer. Ethn.*, pt. 1, pp. 3–195, Washington, 1904.

FLETCHER, ALICE V. The Hako. *Twenty-second Ann. Rept. Bur. Amer. Ethn.*, pt. 2, Washington, 1904.

——— *and* LA FLESCHE, FRANCIS. The Omaha tribe. *Twenty-seventh Ann. Rept. Bur. Amer. Ethn.*, Washington, 1911.

Food products of the North American Indians. In *Report of the Commissioner of Agriculture for 1870*, Washington, 1871.

FRENCH, B. F. Historical collections of Louisiana. Part IV. New York, 1852.

HARIOT, THOMAS. A brief and true report of the new found land of Virginia. Francoforti, 1590. *Reprinted*, New York, 1872.

HARSHBERGER, JOHN W. Phytogeographic influences in the arts and industries of American aborigines. In *Bull. Geog. Soc. Phila.*, vol. IV, no. 3, pp. 25–41. Phila., 1906.

HAVARD, V.   Food plants of the North American Indians.   In *Bull. Torrey Bot. Club*, vol. XXII, no. 3, pp. 98–120, Lancaster, Pa., March, 1895.

HEWITT, J. N. B.   Iroquoian cosmology.   In *Twenty-first Ann. Rept. Bur. Amer. Ethn.*, pp. 127–339, Washington, 1903.

JENKS, ALBERT ERNEST.   The wild rice gatherers of the upper lakes.   In *Nineteenth Ann. Rept. Bur. Amer. Ethn.*, pt. 2, pp. 1019–1137, Washington, 1900.

Jesuit relations and allied documents.   Edited by Reuben Gold Thwaites. Vols. VI, XXXVIII, XLVIII, LIX, LXVIII, Cleveland, 1897–1900.

KALM, PETER.   Travels into North America.   Translated by John Reinhold Forster.   Vols. I–II.   London, 1772.

LA FLESCHE, FRANCIS.   *See* FLETCHER *and* LA FLESCHE.

LA SALLE.   *See* COX, ISAAC, *ed.*

LE PAGE DU PRATZ, ANTOINE S.   Histoire de la Louisiane.   Vols. I–III.   Paris, 1758.

MAXIMILLIAN, ALEX. PHILIPP (Prinz zu Wied).   Reise in das innere Nord-America in den Jahren 1832 bis 1834.   B. I–II.   Coblenz, 1839–1841.

NAUDIN, CH.   Revue des cucurbitacés.   In *Annales des Sciences Naturelles*, 4th ser., vol. XII, Botanique, pp. 79–164, Paris, 1859.

NUTTALL, THOMAS.   Collections towards a flora of the Territory of Arkansas. In *Trans. Amer. Philos. Soc.*, n. s., vol. V, pp. 139–203, Phila., 1837.

Outlook, vol. 104, no. 2, New York, May 10, 1913.

PELZER, LOUIS.   Henry Dodge.   Iowa Biographical Series, State Hist. Soc. Iowa, Iowa City, 1911.

PERROT, NICOLAS.   *See* BLAIR, EMMA, *translator and editor.*

PICKERING, CHARLES.   Chronological history of plants.   Boston, 1879.

PISO, WILLEM.   Historiae naturalis & medicae.   Amsterdam, 1658.

POUND, ROSCOE, *and* CLEMENTS, FREDERIC E.   The phytogeography of Nebraska. I. General Survey.   Lincoln, Neb., 1900.

RIGGS, STEPHEN RETURN.   A Dakota-English dictionary.   *Cont. N. Amer. Ethn.*, vol. VII, Washington, 1890.

RUSSELL, FRANK.   The Pima Indians.   In *Twenty-sixth Ann. Rept. Bur. Amer. Ethn.*, pp. 17–389, Washington, 1908.

STRACHEY, WILLIAM.   The historie of travaile into Virginia Britannia.   Hakluyt Society Pub., vol. VI, London, 1849.

THOMAS, CYRUS.   Report on the mound explorations of the Bureau of Ethnology. *Twelfth Ann. Rept. Bur. Amer. Ethn.*, Washington, 1894.

WATSON, SERENO.   Contributions to American botany.   In *Proc. Am. Acad. Arts and Sciences*, vol. XXII (n. s. XIV), pp. 396–481, Boston, 1887.

WILLIAMSON, JOHN P.   An English-Dakota dictionary.   New York, 1902.

INDEX

119